Praise for *Renatus' Kayak*

"Whether this is the stuff of Hollywood, of ~   ʋ, or fate, it is a story Rozanne Enerson Iᴜⁿˡ

— Jamie Brake, A   ᴧment

"Northern Labrador is a haunted land inhabited by ghosts, memories and the mingled lives of Inuit, Moravian missionaries, fur traders and, for a while during WWII, U.S. servicemen who manned a remote weather station there. Prompted by a model kayak, acquired by her uncle who was stationed at Hebron, Rozanne Enerson Junker has crafted a subtle blending of historical accounts to reveal the complexity of competing personalities and interests. Versatile and quintessential, the kayak was a critical element to the success of Inuit survival. *Renatus' Kayak* carries a heavy burden of the social complexities that have shaped the emergence of Inuit autonomy and governance as well as vestiges of lives now vanished."

— Stephen Loring, Arctic Studies Center, Smithsonian Institution

"The story of Renatus Tuglavina and the secret American weather station in Hebron, Labrador is a story that ought to be told to our children and grandchildren. It is the story of an Inuk who led with courage and determination and wasn't afraid to take a stand for what he believed was right. It is a lost story of the role Hebron played in World War II and a story of how our cultural heritage lives on long after we ourselves have passed."

— Johannes Lampe, President, Nunatsiavut Government

"I would like to first congratulate you on a wonderful piece of work! Thoroughly researched and presented, your book delves into a depth of personal history that we seldom see. This is an important contribution on a number of levels: your own family history, social relationships between Inuit and non-Inuit, Labrador history, wartime history, feelings of the heart, and the story of your own research experiences. [...] You have gifted us all a great story."

– Kenneth R. Lister, Assistant Curator of Anthropology, retired,
Royal Ontario Museum

"Labrador is a remote, unforgiving and fascinating corner of the world, known only to a few. As a sailor visiting outports with the lieutenant Governor of Newfoundland, and as a military historian many years later finding an unmanned German weather station erected in Martin Bay in 1943, I had many unanswered questions. One of these questions was answered when learning from this remarkable book that another secret weather station existed – only this time manned by our Allies, the Americans, and located near the Moravian Mission settlement of Hebron. As someone 'come from away,' Renatus' Kayak provided me a wonderful context in which to better understand Labrador's significant role in the Second World War, how one G.I. was taken under the wing of an Inuit family and how the memories of a single year can last a lifetime."

– W. A. B. (Alec) Douglas, Naval Historian, Ottawa

Renatus' Kayak

A Labrador Inuk, an American G.I. and a Secret World War II Weather Station

Rozanne Enerson Junker

POLAR HORIZONS

Cover design by: Andrej Seminc aka semnitz.
Front cover artwork: Silent Boats #5 by Allen Smutylo, 1992, etching and chine colle, 14" x 32".
Front cover photo: Hebron 1945. Collection of Elwood Belsheim.
Back cover photo: U.S. Weather Station, Hebron 1945. Collection of Elwood Belsheim.
Also appearing on the back cover is the U.S. military badge worn by American servicemen who served in Labrador in WWII.

Published by Polar Horizons Inc.
27 de Cotignac Street
Gatineau Quebec J8T 8E4
info@polarhorizons.com
www.polarhorizons.com/en

ISBN 978-1-7750815-0-0 (paperback), 978-1-7750815-1-7 (epub)

Legal deposit, 2017
Bibliothèque et Archives nationales du Québec
Library and Archives Canada

Cataloguing data available from Library and Archives Canada.

Inuit song

And I think over again
My small adventures
When from a shore wind I drifted out
In my kayak
And I thought I was in danger.
My fears,
Those small ones
That I thought so big,
For all the vital things
I had to get and to reach.
And yet, there is only
One great thing,
The only thing.
To live and see in huts and on journeys
The great day that dawns,
And the light that fills the world.

Kitlinuharmiut Song (Copper Eskimo)
Recorded and translated by Knud Rasmussen
on the Kent Peninsula,
from *The Report of 5th Thule Expedition 1921–1924*

(Brown 2015)

Table of Contents

List of Figures

Foreword

"Our artifacts tell more about ourselves than our confessions."[1]

The Chilean poet, Pablo Neruda, once wrote an elegant statement about a clay sculpture known as "Pretty Woman With Guitar." Sculpted by a ten-year-old girl, the figure symbolizes for the poet the beauty of his native Chile embracing the essence of his homeland.

She has the roundness of hills, of shadows cast by summer clouds on fallow land, and in spite of the fact that she travelled across the seas, she has the renowned odour of clay, of Chilean clay.[2]

In this poetic observation, Neruda reminds us that objects are more than stone, sinew, wood, clay, and bone. Objects belong to technological systems that embody social phenomena. Thus, although a sculpture of clay presents its material aspects and its form, it also embodies the reasons for its creation, the skill of the artist, cultural traditions, its histories and experiences, and the values and emotions of those who admire it and reflect upon its presence.

Rozanne Enerson Junker opens her narrative by introducing us to an Inuit kayak model. The model belonged to her uncle, Woody Belsheim, who acquired it while an American radio operator at a weather station in Hebron, Labrador, during the latter years of World War II. Other than his memories, the kayak model was all that remained to tie her uncle to his Labrador experiences. As we reflect upon Neruda's sculpture, what does Woody Belsheim's kayak then represent? Is it a model showing an example of a summer hunting tool made and used by the Inuit in former times? Is it a teaching tool where the young are taught construction and sewing techniques by observing and listening to the instructions and stories of their elders? Is it a symbol of Inuit identity that ties the Inuit to the land and to the animals upon which they depend? Is it an item of trade—often referred to in the non-Inuit world as a "curiosity"—that was part of the Inuit economy in which Woody Belsheim participated? Is it a tangible reminder—hanging on the walls of Belsheim's California home—of his own isolation, cold, and duty supporting the war effort? With its wood frame and sinew-sewn cover, did it stimulate feelings fonder than duty that haunted Belsheim throughout his life? And in its most recent manifestation, is it the inspiration for a deepened relationship between an uncle and a niece and a research path that led to the unveiling of an American and Canadian story that speaks to Inuit and non-Inuit relationships, love, family, and the physical and emotional distances created by circumstances and the passing of time?

View the photographs of the model in Figures 1, 2, 3, and 68 and we see a wood framed kayak with a sealskin cover. With robust gunwales, hard chines, and a relatively flat bottom, the kayak model has the look of strength and paddling stability. The combing is "floating," held by the skin cover that folds up from beneath and lashed with sealskin rope. Deck straps of sealskin extend over the bow and stern to hold hunting equipment and attest to the kayak's hunting role in Inuit culture. These characteristics are all qualities of the Labrador Inuit kayak. Thus, the kayak model symbolizes the Inuit hunting culture where men and women join their skills in the creation of a tool that helps support the Inuit family and community, as the kayak itself depends upon the materials supplied by the animals hunted.

With unusual foresight, Woody Belsheim noted that the kayak model was made by Renatus Tuglavina of Hebron, dated to 1944. Tuglavina—as described through the research of Junker—was a skilled Inuit hunter and clearly possessed the traditional knowledge necessary for creating an accurate model of a Labrador Inuit kayak. Belsheim likely valued the model as a souvenir as it could be easily transported. But, it also represented well the Inuit culture Belsheim admired. It displayed Inuit relationship to the land and animals, gender division of labour, skill of the hand, traditional knowledge passed down from elder to youth, and perhaps most importantly, his own emotional attachments.

It is the latter point that Junker's in-depth research addresses. Through her narrative we learn of Woody Belsheim's loving relationship with a young Inuit woman—Harriot Tuglavina, daughter of Renatus—whom he met shortly after arriving in Hebron. Brought together by world politics and by community social relationships, they were in turn separated by forces beyond their own control. In the years to follow, perhaps haunted by guilt and a true sense of love, the kayak model was the closest the author's uncle could come to contact with Renatus Tuglavina's daughter. This is the strength of material culture and this is both the explicit and the implicit backdrop to Junker's remarkable story.

For my part, I would have valued sitting down to a conversation with Woody Belsheim. The kayak model, as it became for Rozanne Enerson Junker, would have been a focus. Perhaps he would have thought about the kayak's multitude of associations. And perhaps, with reflection, think about the epigraph and agree with Joseph Brodsky that "Our artifacts tell more about ourselves than our confessions."

Kenneth R. Lister
Assistant Curator of Anthropology, retired
Royal Ontario Museum

August 2017

---

[1] Joseph Brodsky. 1992. *Watermark*. New York: Farrar, Straus, and Giroux, p. 61.

[2] Pablo Neruda. 1984. "A Lady in Clay". In *Pablo Neruda: Passions and Impressions*. Matilda Neruda and Miguel Otero Silva, eds. p. 177. New York: Farrar, Straus and Giroux.

Preface

I HAD SUCCESSFULLY FINISHED a demanding eight-year position in the summer of 2008 and to celebrate its conclusion, I rewarded myself with a "Viking Trails to America" cruise on the icebreaker, *Polar Star*. My great-grandparents were from Norway and Viking lore had always fascinated me. I had read the Icelandic sagas and was looking forward to exploring some of the areas they featured. Unlike those who dream of Bali or Fiji, my dream destination was the North. We sailed from Reykjavik, Iceland, to Brattahlid in South Greenland where we visited Eric the Red's settlement, across the Davis Strait to Baffin Island, down the coast of Labrador to L'Anse aux Meadows on the northern tip of Newfoundland—Helluland, Markland and Vinland to the Vikings. It was L'Anse aux Meadows where the archaeologist Anne Stine Ingstad and her husband, Helge Ingstad, discovered remains of what was to become the first authenticated Viking settlement in the New World.

While exploring the coast of Labrador, which at 113 640 square miles is equal in size to the state of Arizona, but with approximately 5 000 miles of coastline, we stopped at Killiniq Island, Torngat (place of spirits) Mountains National Park, and the once vibrant Moravian mission settlements of Hebron and Ramah, which had been rich hunting areas for Inuit for hundreds of years. I was awed by its stark, isolated beauty.

The next summer, on my way to watch the USA Outdoor Track and Field Championships in Eugene, Oregon, I decided, on a whim, to stop near Red Bluff, California, and visit my aunt and uncle, Ida and Woody Belsheim. Even though Ida was my father's sister, I didn't know her or Woody very well as they had spent most of their married life in Los Angeles and I had grown up in North Dakota. But I had visited them a couple of times in the early 1980s when I worked for Governor Jerry Brown, and I thought it would be nice to say hello again as I would be driving right by their home.

I brought along photos of the Viking trip because I was sure that, being proud Norwegians, they would both appreciate them. Woody could not have cared less. All he asked was "Did you go to Hebron?" I was shocked. I'm ashamed to say that many Americans don't know where Labrador is, much less Hebron. How in the world did Woody?

Woody had been increasingly confined to a wheelchair, but at 87 years old, his mind was sharp and he spent his days on the computer in his home office or reading and working the daily crossword puzzle at the dining room table. But 65 years earlier he had been an American serviceman, one of only seven G.I.'s posted to a secret American weather station in Hebron, Labrador, during World War II. I was fascinated to hear his stories of the War and of the Inuit he knew and, over the next two years, we corresponded by email and letters and I visited him a few more times to try to better understand his adventures in Hebron.

Fig. 1 Woody Belsheim with the sealskin kayak.
(Photo: Rozanne Enerson Junker, 2010)

Of all that Woody had brought back with him from Labrador—
the ivory carvings, the embroidery work, the cribbage boards,
and the sealskin jacket—only a small sealskin kayak model remained, hanging in his den or on his bathroom walls, its tiny
delicate stitching firmly intact. Woody had written in black

marker on the bottom of the kayak, *Made by Reyanastrus Tuglavina of Hebron, Labrador 1944 sealskin.*

Woody told me that he and Reyanastrus' daughter, Harriot, had been "steadies" during the year he spent in Hebron. Harriot Tuglavina and her young son had waited with Woody for the arrival of the U.S. Army seaplane that was taking him back to the United States after his year's service in Hebron. Woody did his best to explain to Harriot, in broken Inuktitut and English, that he needed to go where the army sent him. That he didn't have a choice. He had to leave. He said to me, "What could I do? I wasn't a hunter. I wasn't a sealer." (Belsheim 2010).

But Woody had thought about Harriot over the years and hoped she had found someone to give her a good life. He had found Harriot listed in the online 1935 and 1945 Newfoundland and Labrador censuses, and he had read of the tragic results of the relocation of Hebron's Inuit population in 1959, but he could find nothing specifically related to Harriot or Reyanastrus since Newfoundland and Labrador joined the Canadian Confederation in 1949.

Woody gave me the sealskin kayak model at the end of a two-day videotaping session. I had never seen the kayak before. We had spent the weekend talking about Reyanastrus and Harriot, Woody's training, his army buddies and their lives in the isolated settlement of Hebron. Woody remembered the government trader and his beautiful Inuit wife and he voiced the servicemen's suspicions of the German-speaking Moravian missionaries.

While the string tightly knotting the wooden frame of the model kayak had turned grey and the bow and stern were worn, the stitches in the sealskin were completely intact, and the thin leather straps in front and behind the cockpit that, in a full-sized kayak, would have held the harpoon and other sealing equipment were firmly attached. The cockpit itself was stitched to the sealskin and had once been painted silver.

I felt an enormous responsibility, driving back to San Francisco with the kayak in the back seat of my car. I knew then that I would try to answer Woody's questions about Reyanastrus and Harriot and that, if at all possible, I would return the kayak to Labrador. It was, in my mind, a cultural treasure.

I didn't understand it at the time, but Woody had given me a gift far greater than the kayak. The most precious gift was the people I would meet and the places I would visit, people and places I couldn't have imagined before beginning the search. Each step along the way I was guided by individuals who pointed me in the right direction, including:

- The archivist at Library and Archives Canada who said "Have you contacted Prof. Hans J. Rollmann at Memorial University of Newfoundland?" when I asked to see the Moravian church records for Hebron.
- Prof. Rollmann, who answered my query by saying, "Yes, those records are here in my office." It was also there that I found that the correct spelling for Reyanastrus was Renatus. Prof. Rollmann has been a

tremendous source of additional material regarding Hebron in the 1930s and 1940s.

- Aimee Chaulk, editor of *Them Days* in Happy Valley-Goose Bay, who, when I mentioned Carol Brice-Bennett's seminal work on Inuit relocation and my difficulty contacting her, said offhandedly "Oh! Carol, she lives just up the street!"

- Carol Brice-Bennett, who, when I told her what I was searching for, asked "What took you so long to find me?"

- The desk clerk at Atsanik Lodge in Nain, Labrador, who, when I asked her how I might locate Ernestina Tuglavina, Renatus' granddaughter, in the town of 1 000 people, said "Oh! That shouldn't be a problem. Her daughter Paula works here. She'll be at breakfast in the morning."

- Elias "Jerry" Tuglavina, whom I first met in 2008 when he was doing carpentry work at the dilapidated Hebron mission, only to discover in 2011 that he was the son of Woody's best friend, the American serviceman, cook and carpenter Hank Bradley, and Renatus' niece, Hulda Tuglavina.

- Irene Frieda, the woman who cooked breakfast at the Amaguk Inn in Hopedale, who turned out to be the daughter of John and Eugenia Piercy, the storekeepers in Hebron who Woody had known. I had a photo of her parents that Woody had taken in 1944 in my room.

- Peter Evans, PhD, whom I contacted after reading a 10-year-old edition of *Kinatuinamut Ilingajuk* magazine featuring a story of the 1959 Hebron relocation. Peter told me that Renatus Tuglavina had led an Inuit rebellion against the Hudson's Bay Company post in Hebron in 1933. He suggested getting hold of the 1958 book *Challenger* which described the events.

- British Royal Navy Rear-Admiral George Stephen Ritchie, author of *Challenger* (whom I contacted in Scotland via British Telecom when I couldn't find his obituary), who said, when asked about his source material for the Renatus Tuglavina story, "You'll have to speak louder, I'm 97 years old!" A few days later Ritchie gave me the address of a Captain Michael Baker in Devon, England, who he thought could help me.

- Michael Baker and Rupert Baker, the son and grandson of Lieutenant-Commander E. H. B. "Buck" Baker, who generously shared Baker's hand-written, private Labrador diary and allowed me to photograph his picture album, which I hadn't known existed.

This serendipitous guidance at critical points in the research made me feel that the story of Renatus Tuglavina, Woody Belsheim, and the sealskin kayak was one I had been chosen to tell.

Finally, it should be noted that the kayak featured in *Silent Boat #5* on the cover of *Renatus' Kayak* is a Greenlandic kayak and not a North Labrador kayak. Although I don't claim to understand the differences between the two, I do know that shape, size and fittings differ. Rather than strive for authenticity in the kayak's cover design, I opted to use an artwork that encapsulated the essence of the story—a kayak, a hunter and a young woman. The ominous presence lurking in the upper right hand corner might represent the unknown or perhaps it is a foreshadowing of things to come? There is the golden light of summer and the cold darkness of winter. The orange X's, as with the entire work, is open to interpretation. Are they stitching on the kayak or clothing, or is it the coming of the church? I leave it to your imagination.

Acknowledgments

I AM GRATEFUL FOR THE HELP and hospitality extended to me by so many people in Happy Valley-Goose Bay, Hopedale, Nain, Ottawa, and St. John's, Canada, and Devon, England. Special thanks to: Kathy Anstett, Tom Artiss, Christine Baikie, Capt. Michael Baker, Rupert and Elaine Baker, Ida Belsheim, Jamie Brake, Carol Brice-Bennett, Ron Boring, Wallace Broomfield, Anne Budgell, Aimee Chaulk, Dr. W. A. B. (Alec) Douglas, Peter Evans, Johanna (Hannie) Hettasch Fitzgerald, David Igloliorte, Philip Igloliorte, John Jararuse, Sem and Hulda (Tuglavina) Kajuatsiak, Marlene Kenney, Lynn Lafontaine, Sarah Leo, Annie Lidd, Dave Lough, Bonnie and George Lyall, Martha MacDonald, Laura Eugenia Millie, Jane Naisbitt, Stonia Nochasak, Gordon Obed Sr., Scott Osmond, Eddie Pottle, Joan Ritcey, Rear-Admiral George Stephen Ritchie, Prof. Hans J. Rollmann, Gustav Semigak, Hulda Semigak, Angus Simpson, Ian Tamblyn, Henoche Townley, Sarah Townley, Ernestina Tuglavina and her daughter Paula, Jerry Tuglavina and his daughter Gwen, Sabina (Tuglavina) Winters, Sophie Tuglavina, and Linda White. Thanks also to

Howard Junker for his continued support. A special thanks to artist and author Allen Smutylo for his generous permission to use *Silent Boats #5* on the cover of *Renatus' Kayak*. Working with my publisher, France Rivet of Polar Horizons, has been a terrific experience. Her expertise and attention to detail as well as her kindness and generosity of spirit, brought the story of *Renatus' Kayak* to light.

I am also grateful for the help of these institutions: Canadian War Museum Archives, Ottawa; Hettasch Collection, Library and Archives Canada, Ottawa; Hettasch Family Collection, Memorial University of Newfoundland, St. John's; OkâlaKatiget Society Archives, Nain; Hudson's Bay Company Collection, Archives of Manitoba, Winnipeg; Moravian Mission Records: Periodical Reports, Hebron and Killinek Church Books, The Rooms Corporation of Newfoundland and Labrador, St. John's; Labrador Institute, Happy Valley-Goose Bay; and Them Days Archives, Happy Valley-Goose Bay.

With the help of these people and these institutions, I have been able to piece together the story that was launched by the kayak Renatus made and gave to Woody, and Woody entrusted to me.

Main Characters

The family of Renatus Tuglavina:

Renatus Tuglavina: Inuk hunter. Father of Paulina, Harriot, Josef Richard, Hulda and Sabina Rhoda. Maker of model sealskin kayak. Son of Tuglavina (Old Tuglavi and Arnatuk. Born near Killinek, Quebec, in 1896. Brother of Josef and Jonas (also called *James* in HBC post journals).

Loida Semigak Tuglavina Henoche: Wife of Renatus. Daughter of Anatsiak and Paniguniak. Granddaughter of Semigak of Nachvak Fjord. Born in 1889. Mother of Paulina, Harriot, Josef Richard, Hulda and Sabina Rhoda.[3]

Paulina Tuglavina: Renatus and Loida's first child. Mother to:

> *Ernestina Jararuse:* who would marry Joe K. A. Tuglavina, her first cousin (Harriot Tuglavina's son).

Tabea Harriot Tuglavina: Renatus and Loida's second child. Girlfriend of American G.I. Elwood "Woody" Belsheim. Mother of:

> *Josef Kefas Andreas Tuglavina (Joe K. A.):* Adopted by Renatus and Loida Tuglavina and later raised by Sabina and Johannes Tuglavina. (Sabina was Loida's sister.)

> *Lena Louisa Elsie Dina Tuglavina:* Adopted by Sabina and Johannes Tuglavina.

> *Dina Harriot Maggie Paulina Elizabeth Semigak:* Harriot's first child with husband, Martin Semigak.

> *Jonas Gustave Thomas Semigak:* Harriot's second child with husband, Martin Semigak.

Elwood "Woody" Belsheim: American G.I. U.S. Army Airways Communications System (AACS) radio operator stationed in Hebron, Labrador, 1944–1945. Taken under the wing of the Renatus Tuglavina family while in Hebron.

Other members of Hebron, Labrador, community (1933–1948):

Lieutenant-Commander E. H. B. "Buck" Baker: Head of the British Royal Navy's survey team in Labrador, 1933–1934. Put Renatus Tuglavina under house arrest in 1934.

Leonard Budgell: HBC employee who knew Renatus Tuglavina and wrote about him in *Them Days.*

F. C. Paul Grubb: Moravian missionary in Hebron when the first Americans arrived in 1943.

Siegfried and Frieda Hettasch: Moravian missionaries while Woody was in Hebron.

John and Eugenia Piercy: Hebron storekeepers, Northern Labrador Trading Organization.

Elias "Jerry" Tuglavina: Son of American G.I. Hank Bradley and Hulda Tuglavina, daughter of Elias and Henrietta Tuglavina. Born in Hebron, 1945.

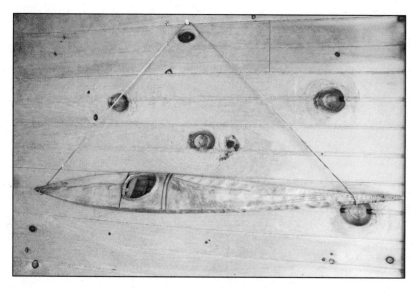

Fig. 2 Renatus' model kayak.
(Photo: Rozanne Enerson Junker, 2017)

Fig. 3 Woody's writing under the kayak.
It reads "Made by Reyanastrus Tuglavina of Hebron, Labrador 1944 sealskin."
(Photo: Rozanne Enerson Junker, 2017)

---

[3] According to Sabina Rhoda's daughter and granddaughter, Sabina always spelled her middle name Roda. The Moravian records show Rhoda.

Introduction

MANY SUCH SEALSKIN KAYAK MODELS exist today. Some older, some newer. Some in better condition than others. Some with harpoons and hunting tools and some without. Several came to the States as souvenirs packed away in the duffle bags of American servicemen upon their return from Labrador. Like older photographs of Inuit or carvings done by Inuit, the artist or the subject is unknown. They are simply *Inuit*.

But this kayak is different. It has provenance. And that's what makes it special. From Woody, we learned that it was made in Hebron, Labrador, by an Inuk named Renatus Tuglavina in the mid-1940s. In the process of trying to find Renatus and his daughter, Harriot, I uncovered bits and pieces of their lives. Sharing their stories ultimately puts this sealskin kayak in context; it is the purpose of this book.

It began, at its most basic, as a love story. Woody was nearing the end of his life and he had unanswered questions about the young Inuit woman, Harriot, he had known and loved during World War II. A constant reminder, the sealskin kayak that her father had given him, never far away. He felt conflicted, guilty perhaps, that he left this young woman when his tour of duty was up and he was sent back to the States. He had heard later that she had taken his loss "pretty hard." He didn't say so at the time, but I've come to believe that he wanted reassurance that things had turned out okay for her; that, in his words, she had found a man who could give her a good life.

While searching mid-century historical records for Renatus and Harriot, I learned that within this small community of Hebron were a diverse group of people with highly varied backgrounds: Moravian missionaries were there to bring Inuit to Christ through education and religious training; Newfoundland Rangers were there to enforce game laws, distribute aid, and keep the peace; Northern Labrador government employees were there to trade fish and furs for sundries like flour, tea and tobacco to Inuit, having taken over the business from the Hudson's Bay Company two years earlier; and Inuit families, some who lived near the mission and others who stayed in summer and winter camps away from the mission. It is into this community that the seven American servicemen were sent—to take weather measurements, code them and transmit the readings south as part of the war effort.

Renatus, as it turned out, was mentioned in three published books, numerous magazine and newspaper articles, and was the subject of a number of high-level government missives between the British Admiralty and the Commission of Government, which governed Newfoundland and Labrador from 1934 to 1949.

This story reflects a tiny moment in history. A moment that in the big picture probably means very little, but to the people who lived it, it meant the world. Not unlike each of our own lives.

As a final note, I would like to say that much of the material quoted in the story that follows is, seen with today's eyes, racist and condescending regarding the Inuit's way of life. The irony is, of course, that in spite of that, it is a tale of Inuit strength, resilience and ingenuity.

Fig. 4 Torngat Mountains.
(Photo: Rozanne Enerson Junker, 2011)

Fig. 5 Torngat Mountains near Hebron, Labrador.
(Photo: Rozanne Enerson Junker, 2011)

CHAPTER 1

Labrador in World War II: Setting the Stage

WORLD WAR II CHANGED LABRADOR FOREVER. From the earliest Viking explorers to latter-day adventurers like Mina Hubbard, Labrador had attracted more than its share of international attention. Basque, French, British, Dutch and American fishermen exploited Labrador's natural maritime resources for hundreds of years. The Hudson's Bay Company traded in the fur of beaver, mink, seal, foxes, and bears. Moravian missionaries arrived in the late 1770s to bring Inuit to Christ. Archaeological, anthropological and scientific expeditions had come and gone, searching for the past and in the case of geologists, perhaps the future. The race to the North Pole had touched down. But World War II was different.

Birth of the Ferry Command

With the coming of American military bases, in support of World War II and later the Cold War, Labrador began to host *in situ* a rather large number of transient foreigners for an extended length of time. At sites like Goose Bay, the air force brought money. People who had never held a salaried job before found work in construction. There were movie nights at the installation in Hopedale. Gallon cans of food were shared with the locals. Airfields and landing strips were built, access to medical services, especially in emergencies, became more readily available and communication with the outside world was improved.

Why Labrador? First, because it was the shortest route to take when transporting airplanes from North America to the European continent. And, secondly, Baffin Island, Greenland and Iceland were convenient stopping-off areas should aircrafts need to refuel or if the weather became too bad to fly. This movement of planes from Labrador and Newfoundland—over 10 000 in all—was critical to the war effort.

The British had declared war on Germany on September 3, 1939, two days after Germany invaded Poland. Mackenzie King, the Prime Minister of Canada, issued a proclamation of support for the British on September 3, and on September 10, the Canadian Parliament declared war on Germany. The United States didn't officially enter World War II until two years later, December 8, 1941, a day after the Japanese bombed Pearl Harbor, Hawaii. Within the next three days, Germany and Italy declared war on the United States and the United States responded in kind.

Prior to Pearl Harbor, President Roosevelt had persuaded the U.S. Congress to support British and French efforts against the Germans by repealing the arms embargo provisions of the Neutrality Acts that had been passed in the 1930s in an attempt to keep the U.S. out of foreign conflicts after World War I. He had also met secretly with Winston Churchill in August 1941, in Newfoundland, to develop a format for post-war political and economic relationships that ultimately laid the groundwork for the United Nations (Flanagan 2015: 37). After the fall of France in June 1940, Roosevelt declared that the U.S must become "the great arsenal of democracy." (Roosevelt 1940). American industry would be put to work producing thousands of airplanes, tanks, ships and munitions for itself and its allies.

Building aircraft was one thing. Delivering them to Britain in a safe, timely, and economical manner was another. Initially, planes had been assembled on the West Coast, flown to the East Coast, taken apart, crated, loaded onto ships, and sent across the Atlantic only to be unloaded and reassembled before being flown into combat. As the war intensified, this process took too much time and the planes couldn't be delivered in the numbers the war demanded. In addition, German submarines scouring the Atlantic were making it more difficult than ever to bring planes across safely on ships.

The idea of flying warplanes across the Atlantic to supply the Allies' needs was a radical one. In the twenty years before the outbreak of World War II, less than a hundred successful

Atlantic crossings had been made. Fifty flights had failed because of "rough weather, engine problems, or overloading." (Christie 1995: 3).

Britain's Royal Air Force (RAF) didn't believe it could be done on a scale needed to win the war. Distances were too large, ocean skies too dangerous, crews too inexperienced, and there were too few trained pilots. Neither communications nor weather infrastructure were in place to support such flights. And even if there were, the ravages of a northern winter simply made it impossible (Ibid.: 26–27).

But it was a thought that intrigued Ontario-born and New Brunswick-raised William Maxwell "Max" Aitken, the First Baron Beaverbrook, Prime Minister Winston Churchill's Minister of Aircraft Production. Aitken, a former newspaperman, understood the power of ideas to capture the imagination and undertook to make the delivery of planes by air a reality. He argued that if Britain were to win the "war of machines," it would have to take the gamble (Time 1940).

The first implementers of what was to become known as the Ferry Command were civilians, as the British Air Ministry and the Royal Air Force refused to spare any aircrew to test the idea. Some men were recruited from the British Overseas Airways Corporation (BOAC), but the majority were American and Canadian volunteer pilots, radiomen, and navigators.

The United States was still a neutral country at this time and providing planes to a nation at war violated its neutrality laws. To get around the problem, Lockheed Hudson bombers were flown from their factories in Los Angeles up to the Canadian border and then hauled across by horses or tractors.

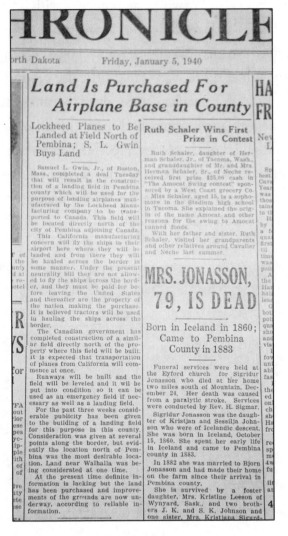

Fig. 6 *Cavalier Chronicle*, January 5, 1940.
Report on the purchase of land for the purpose of building a landing strip for the war planes. (Photo: Rozanne Enerson Junker)

The Cavalier Chronicle reported a bomber being dragged across the border on January 19, 1940. It wasn't a secret. Over 200 people watched as two large bombers with 60-foot wingspans landed on a cleared piece of farmland north of the town of Pembina, North Dakota, a few hours from Woody's hometown. While there was some difficulty getting the pilots through customs, they finally received permission to enter Canada. The airplane engines had to be turned off so that the horses could pull them, tails first, 100 feet across the border. As the temperature was -15 °F (-26 °C), it was imperative to restart the engines as soon as possible to get the planes on their way immediately (Cavalier Chronicle 1940b).

Fig. 7 *Cavalier Chronicle*, January 19, 1940.
The photo's caption reads: "The plane pictured above is one of two United States manufactured bombing planes that were hauled across the border to Canada at Pembina Monday afternoon. It is stated the planes cost $100,000."
(Photo: Rozanne Enerson Junker)

The first flight test of the Ferry Command took place on November 10, 1940, when seven Lockheed Hudsons carried 22 British, Canadian, American, and Australian pilots, co-pilots, navigators and radio operators from Gander, Newfoundland, across the North Atlantic to the Royal Air Force airfield at Aldergrove, Northern Ireland. Flights had never been made this late in the season before. The goal was to fly in formation, at night, without navigational lights. All seven planes landed safely, with the men sucking oxygen through simple tubes while flying at 18 000 feet. They had approximately three hours on land before being shuttled onto a ship returning to Canada the next day (Christie 1995: 49–60).

Two basic flight routes were developed. The northern one was designed for fighters, light and medium bombers and all other planes with one or two engines. Aircrafts left Montréal, Quebec, refuelled in Goose Bay, Labrador, Narssarssuak, Greenland, and Reykjavik, Iceland, before arriving in Prestwick, Scotland. The southern route was intended for larger, four-engine planes and began at Presque Isle, Maine, with a stop in Gander, Newfoundland, and then a non-stop flight over the ocean to Prestwick, Scotland (Shores 1947: 52).

While it had been shown that these North Atlantic flights were possible, it was still extremely dangerous and by the end of the war 500 men had perished. One of the first casualties was Sir Frederick Banting, the Nobel Prize-winning Canadian scientist who co-discovered insulin. Dr. Banting was studying the physical effects of high altitude travel and was on board to test a newly designed antigravity flying suit. The Hudson he was in crash-landed in a rugged area of Newfoundland while attempting to return to Gander after engine trouble, and Dr. Banting died of wounds suffered in the accident and exposure. (Christie 1995: 62–72).

Army Airways Communication System

Even with these losses, the experiment was declared a success and work was begun to build the radio communications and weather measurement and dissemination infrastructure necessary to support an effort that would ultimately result in over 11 000 planes being flown across the Atlantic (Ibid.: 305). That job fell to the Army Airways Communication System (AACS) that had been created in 1938 as part of the U.S. Army Air Corps. In April 1941, approximately five months after the first successful flight to Aldergrove, five AACS servicemen sailed to St. John's, Newfoundland, and then on to Gander to set up the first AACS facility outside of the United States. Their job: to "build highways in the sky." (Shores 1947: 33)

The AACS' mission was to create a 24-hour ground-to-air radio connectivity that would provide fast, accurate and systematized point-to-point flight messaging while at the same time successfully hiding those dispatches from the enemy. With radio connectivity, pilots could signal distress and would have access to critical meteorological information that would allow them to predict weather patterns and make decisions accordingly. Such information was also used at the front end, to schedule and route delivery of airplanes to Britain. Much has been written about the weather-collection stations code-named Crystal One, Crystal Two, and Crystal Three in Quebec and on Baffin Island,[4] (Ibid.: 38–42; Craven 1955; Smith 2009: 2–4), but the one in Hebron, Labrador, which was in operation for three years and where Woody served, has not been mentioned in any of the AACS histories.

Building these highways in the sky required permission from three countries—Great Britain, Canada and the Commission of Government, which was in charge of Newfoundland. A British Dominion since 1907, Newfoundland and Labrador had been granted full legal freedom in all areas in 1931 and had, for a few years, existed as an independent state within the British Commonwealth on the same level as Canada, Australia and New Zealand. But the Wall Street crash of 1929 and the disruption of markets for its fish and paper exports resulted in a national debt that couldn't be supported. Canada did not have the ability to provide significant, on-going economic aid to Newfoundland, so a British-appointed Royal Commission recommended the suspension of Newfoundland's constitution in 1933, and in February 1934, Newfoundland relinquished self-government. A seven-person Commission of Government was created. It consisted of three British members responsible for the outward-facing, economic and finance-related departments of Natural Resources, Public Utilities, and Finance; three Newfoundlanders were placed in charge of the more inward-facing areas of Justice, Public Health and Welfare, and Home Affairs and Education. All commissioners were appointed by Britain, including the Commission's Governor,

Admiral Sir David Murray Anderson. The Commission was responsible for making as well as carrying out laws.

Canada was a player in this discussion as it had assumed responsibility for the military protection of Newfoundland and Labrador at the beginning of the war when Canadian Prime Minister Mackenzie King stated to the Canadian Parliament that "the integrity of Newfoundland and Labrador is essential to the security of Canada. By contributing as far as we are able to the defence of Newfoundland ... we will not only be defending Canada but we will also be assisting Great Britain." (Higgins 2006). After the fall of France in June 1940, but prior to the U.S. entering the war in December 1941, Americans began negotiations for permission to site military installations in Canada and Labrador. Approval was granted September 1940, "freely and without consideration" (Dzuiban 1959: 164).

The Commission agreed to weather, radio and emergency outposts at Fort Chimo (now Kuujjuaq, Nunavik, Quebec), Frobisher Bay (near Iqaluit, Nunavut on Baffin Island) and Padloping Island (also in Nunavut, along the Davis Strait) in August 1941 (Ibid.: 184). Captain Elliott Roosevelt, an intelligence officer with the U.S. Army Air Force, and President Franklin Roosevelt's son, did the initial surveying of these sites.

But later in the War they found that they needed additional coverage, and in mid-June 1943, the American Consul General in Newfoundland, George D. Hopper, asked Sir Wilfrid W. Woods, Commissioner for Public Utilities, for permission to construct another weather station farther south, at Hebron, requiring an acre or so of land (Hopper 1943, TRC). Approval to build was given by the Commission on July 3, 1943, for the duration of hostilities plus six months. "These installations are part of a general communications and weather reporting program of vital assistance to the war effort, particularly in aiding the Ferry Command," wrote Commissioner Woods (Woods 1943, TRC).

In addition to weather collection and dissemination, two other reasons have been suggested for the U.S. interest in stationing a small contingent of servicemen in Hebron.

On April 9, 1943, two months prior to Hopper's request, Inuit hunters from Hebron found the remains of four American B-26 crewmen who had taken off from Greenland on December 10, 1942, but hadn't been heard from again. Bad weather had forced their plane to land the same day it took off. Search aircraft looked for the missing flyers for weeks before giving them up as lost at sea. The B-26 was hundreds of miles off course. The crew survived for almost two months on rations they allocated sparingly. They radioed for help, but their transmissions were never heard in Goose Bay, Newfoundland, or at any other point. The diary kept by the men described their heroic efforts to live, making their deaths all the more tragic. They were downed near Saglek Bay, less than a four-hour walk from Hebron. If there had been radiomen in Hebron, their calls for help would have been heard (Neely 1968).

The second reason was an unconfirmed suspicion that the Moravian missionaries in Labrador could be German sympathizers. During World War I, Karl Filschke, the German-born Moravian missionary at Killinek who had served in Labrador for 19 years, was considered a German sympathizer and he and his family were deported on Christmas Day 1916. Filschke was interned at Alexandra Palace in London until the end of World War I, after which they were sent to Germany and, despite his requests, were not allowed to return to Labrador (Bassler 2014: 154–156, 166). The current missionaries, who also spoke German, were under suspicion. Former Superintendent of Moravian missions, F. W. Peacock, wrote in early 1982 that "even as late as 1940 there were rumours in Newfoundland that those German missionaries on the coast of Labrador had a gasoline dump with which to supply German U-boats, during the First World War!!! Interesting but absolutely without foundation." (Peacock 1982, CWM).

Newfoundland Ranger Frank G. Mercer was also suspicious of the German influence in Labrador. "One midsummer's day in the late 1930s, the Ranger at Hebron [speaking of himself] observed quantities of German liquor, cigarettes and tobacco in the village; the goods appeared overnight out of the blue. The occurrence coincided with the natives' return from their annual char fishing expedition to Saglek Bay farther north.

"But while it was established the contraband had been obtained from ships of German registry, it was not possible at the time to determine why the ships were in the area. The young Ranger, cut off from the outside by distance, with no communications save one overland mail by dogsled and two by boat yearly, little dreamed then that he had unwittingly stumbled on evidence of the Nazi presence." (Mercer 1972, CWM).

Germany's Unmanned Weather Station in Labrador

Like the Allies, Germany realized the strategic importance of understanding northern weather patterns and sought to establish weather stations throughout the Arctic. Those in Greenland and Iceland were ultimately discovered and destroyed by the Allies or dismantled by the Germans before they could be attacked, but the unmanned one they erected in northern Labrador remained hidden until the early 1980s.

Siemens, the German industrial giant, had developed a battery that could withstand severe cold, making it possible for the men of U-boat 537 to put up a weather station at Martin Bay, near Cape Chidley, on October 23, 1943. The station was put into service just months after the first Americans arrived in Hebron and was disguised with "Canadian Meteor Service" markings, the name of a fictitious governmental department meant to fool the curious (Douglas 1982: 42–47).

The German's nicknamed the weather station "Kurt" after meteorologist Kurt Sommermeyer, who was on board U-boat 537. The weather station reported the barometric pressure, temperature, wind velocity and direction every three hours, in two-minute transmissions. U-boats along the Labrador coast picked up the dispatch and relayed the information to meteorologists in the German Naval Command with an estimated 50% to 60% reliability rate. Researchers generally believe that the unmanned station worked for two to three weeks, although some say two to three months (Ibid.: 46; Clarke No date, CWM).

Fig. 8 German U-boat 537 in Martin Bay, Labrador.
(CWM 20030149-001_2. George Metcalf Archival Collection. Canadian War Museum)

There is some suggestion that the Allies may have intercepted these signals, but didn't know what they were hearing (Ibid.: 46). The most likely reason it took almost 40 years to discover this disguised weather station in the Arctic is that U-boat 537, with its Captain Peter Schrewe and its crew of 58 men, was sunk in the Java Sea just north of Bali by the USS *Flounder* on November 10, 1944 (Wikipedia 2017a). The Germans made another attempt to erect a second weather station in Labrador a year later, but the U-boat 867 carrying the necessary materials was sunk in September 1944 near Bergen, Norway, and no further tries were made (Uboat.net 2017).

Dr. W. A. B. (Alec) Douglas, Director of the Directorate of History, Canada's National Defence Headquarters, was contacted in 1980 by Austrian-born researcher Franz Selinger. Selinger eventually convinced Douglas that they would find the remains of an unmanned German weather station in Martin Bay.

Fig. 9 Unmanned German weather station, Martin Bay, 1981.
(CWM 20030149-001_5. George Metcalf Archival Collection Canadian War Museum)

Selinger and Douglas' 1981 trip to northern Labrador proved Selinger correct in his calculations (Douglas 1982: 42). That the Germans would, in 1943, place a weather station 100 miles north of the manned one recently established in Hebron by the Americans was beyond belief—neither one of them knowing of the other.

Douglas served in the Royal Canadian Navy for 22 years and spent an additional 20 years at National Defence Headquarters.

He was a volunteer at the Canadian War Museum's Military History Research Centre when I met him in May 2010. It was news to him that there had been a secret American weather station at Hebron.

Douglas thought it was possible that the Germans had gotten some of their meteorological information from old Moravian files housed in Germany as the Moravians were voracious record keepers, but he felt that "surely if they had been getting intelligence from them they would have known, which they did not, that when they went to lay their weather station down in Martin Bay it was the one time in the year that the Inuit did their seal hunt about a mile or two away from where they were." (Douglas 2011).

A weather training manual published by the U.S. Army Air Force after the war expressed most poetically the mission of the seven weathermen and radio operators that were stationed in Hebron: "Man is a creature of the atmosphere not of the land; it is in the atmosphere that he lives and of the atmosphere that he breathes. What is more important here, however, is that man flies in the atmosphere—in an airplane through fickle and often treacherous air, in ships buffeted by strange seas and violent storms, in trucks, tanks, and on foot across terrain which is molded by the flow of wind and water. The observation and prediction of that flow of wind and water is the business of the weather services ... for training flights, ferry missions, strategic and tactical bomber missions, and aerial patrols ... . The responsibility for the fulfillment of the mission, then, ultimately rested with the men who observed, analyzed, and forecast weather in the field, whether they were in Alabama or Italy, Iceland or Burma." (Walters 1952).

Or, Hebron, Labrador. 58.2000°N, 62.4000°W.

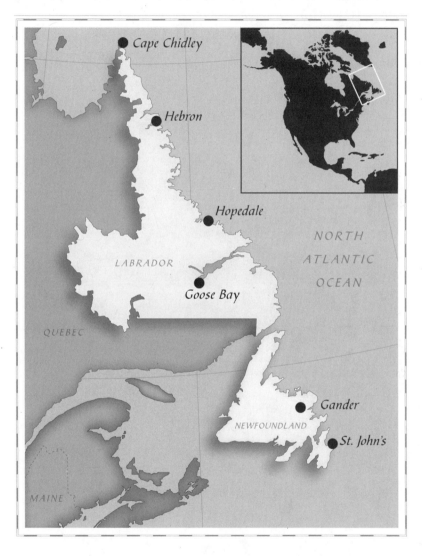

Fig. 10 Various WWII sites in Newfoundland and Labrador.
(Illustration: Diane Mongeau)

---

[4] Fort Chimo was *Crystal I*, the Frobisher Bay Air Base (which became Iqalu-it's commercial/civilian airport) was *Crystal II*, and the station on Padloping Island was *Crystal III*.

CHAPTER 2

Elwood "Woody" Belsheim: An American G.I.

BEING RAISED ON AN ISOLATED FARM outside of Turtle Lake, North Dakota, during the height of the Depression served Woody well in Hebron.

As a newborn, Woody hadn't been expected to live, but he was put into the cook-stove oven of his aunt's farmhouse to keep warm nonetheless. When he was 10 years old his mom, a schoolteacher, died suddenly, most likely of a brain embolism. The next few days were traumatic for Woody. Relatives offered to take his brothers home with them, but it seemed that no one wanted him. "At the time, I guess I thought nobody loved me." (Belsheim 2010).[5]

But then he had a dream and the message he received was plain. "I'm walking along an aunt and uncle's lake with my best friend, our German Shepherd dog. He was walking in front of me when he suddenly sat down, put his nose up, and began that long wolf-like howl (he howled the same way when Mom died). It finally attracted my eyes toward the heaven and there was Jesus. He was holding open a trap door gazing down at me. Our eyes met for several seconds and then he closed the trap door. Without hearing a word, the message I got was clear: He loved me."

Fig. 11 Woody playing a baritone horn in high school.
(Collection of Elwood Belsheim)

Woody was big for his age, six feet tall by the time he was 13. His father had found a woman to come in as hired help after his mother died. Woody mused that his dad probably married her so he wouldn't have to keep paying her wages. She died while Woody was still in high school.

He helped on the family farm, without pay, until he finished high school and after that he went to work as a hired man for one of the local farmers, who offered to pay him a dollar a day plus room and board. After six weeks, he asked for a draw on his wages to go to a dance. His employer gave him $10 and said "That's for October. I pay you less during the winter months and will make it up to you in the spring." At that point, Woody gave notice. Three weeks later he joined the Civilian Conservation Corps and spent the winter in Sioux Falls, South Dakota, before being offered another farmhand position. This time the pay would be 160 acres.

A quarter section of land was a generous proposition, a pretty good deal, but Woody had a buddy who had an uncle that was driving out to Los Angeles, and the temptation to leave the Dakotas for sunny Southern California was just too great. He headed west in the summer of 1941, not quite 18 years old, and never looked back.

Woody's right arm had been mangled when he fell off a pickup truck as a young boy and it was caught underneath. He spent many months in hospital and while the doctors saved the arm, there was a significant loss of movement. Even so, he was able to get a job in the construction business as soon as he arrived in Los Angeles, building bomb shelters to protect planes at the Los Angeles International Airport.

He was eventually hired by Morrison Knutson, the Idaho company that had a contract to construct war relocation centres, also known as internment camps, after President Roosevelt's Executive Order 9066 (Roosevelt 1942, USNA) in February 1942 authorized and directed the Secretary of War to move Americans of Japanese descent from sensitive military locations on the West Coast to inland camps. He helped to build the Tule Lake War Relocation Centre, near Newell, California; Minidoka War Relocation Center close to Eden, Idaho; and the Topaz War Relocation Center next to Delta, Utah. All three are now National Historic Landmarks.

U.S. Army Air Corps Training

Woody had registered for the draft on Valentine's Day 1942, two months after Pearl Harbor. He was just 20 years old. The U.S. Navy had twice rejected him because of his arm, saying there was "no way I could get into any branch of the service." Yet, he was determined to serve.

It was when he was working on the Topaz Camp in Utah that he received notice, on a Wednesday, to report to the U.S. Army Air Corps induction centre in Los Angeles on Friday. He and a buddy drove to Los Angeles and while the army offered to release him after his physical, Woody declined. "It wasn't that I was incapable, I just had a handicap."

Woody took basic training in St. Petersburg, Florida, before being transferred to radio mechanics school in Sioux Falls, South Dakota. There he showed an aptitude for Morse code and, based on his performance, he was sent to Truax Field in Madison, Wisconsin, where he learned to type, code and decode simultaneously. The graduation ceremony for the 600 radio operators was held at the University of Wisconsin and Woody was one of the top five G.I.'s honoured onstage. His military occupation skill (MOS) was as a radio operator with the Army Airways Communication System (AACS). He wasn't incapable, he just had a handicap.

Fig. 12 Woody at basic training in Florida.
(Collection of Elwood Belsheim)

After graduation, Woody was stationed at the Army Air Force Training Center in Smyrna, Tennessee. He was then sent to the Tucson Army Air Field, known as Davis-Monthan Airport and frequented earlier by Charles Lindbergh, Amelia Earhart, and Jimmy Doolittle (Wikipedia 2017b), near Tucson, Arizona. He enjoyed his work at Tucson AAF: "I could sit there by myself with earphones on and I could put half of the stations in one ear and the other half in the other ear. And when my station got a call, I just switched it to one ear and took the message. I could really do that stuff." The U.S. Army then decided to move him from the Tucson desert location and send him to the Arctic.

Arctic training headquarters were at Echo Lake Lodge (elevation, 10 600 feet), at the foot of Mount Evans, Colorado, 45 miles west Denver. After orientation, the servicemen headed out in groups of seven. "From that day on, until the last day, we were just seven of us. It was a big test to see how we got along." Arctic training, Woody said, lost about 20% of the enlistees: "They would go clear off their rockers from loneliness, you know ... but it didn't bother me much because I was alone a lot on the farm."

For six weeks or so they lived in tents and paired off to do chores like cooking, cleaning and building fires. They learned to handle dog teams and sleds. Their last big test was to climb Mount Evans—at 14 271 feet, it would be an elevation gain of 3 600 feet—which is quite difficult when you start at over 10 000 feet. They left from Beaver Meadows through a driving snowstorm. "You could see only so far because you get above the timber line and then it's just pretty wicked. There was a big stone marker there, so you wouldn't lose your way, but if you went over that stone, you'd drop a hundred yards or more. And by then, you needed to rest because you're all winded."

Fig. 13 Arctic dog sled training, Echo Park, Colorado.
(Collection of Elwood Belsheim, 1944)

Mount Evans is one of the rare places where arctic tundra can be found south of the Arctic Circle. Unlike alpine tundra common throughout Colorado, arctic tundra has the ability to hold water once the snow melts (Wilderness.net 2017). Not that this mattered to the men as they trained during the winter months.

The *Them Days* archive in Happy Valley-Goose Bay had a training manual dated July 1, 1943, that was published by the U.S. Military's Arctic, Desert and Tropic Information Center at Eglin Field, Florida. The guide assured military personnel who were lost in the Arctic that they could survive "even if you have only a pocket knife and a few other odds and ends, you can improvise the means for staying alive, if you keep your wits and use them." (Air University (U.S.) 1943: 43, TDA).

The manual suggests making an SOS signal by stamping down the snow with boots and filling the letters with dark brush or moss, if available. If the men begin to sweat, they are advised to take off their clothes "strip to the waist, even in zero weather," but are then warned against "exposing yourself for a long time," as the sun can burn "fiercely" (Ibid.).

"Eskimos, Aleuts, and other northern people" were said to be friendly and servicemen were encouraged to "treat them fairly, show good spirit, and make your needs known as best you can." (Ibid.: 44). It is unclear whether Woody's trainers used this as a source, but it is a possibility. The manual made no mention of *perlerorneq* (Jenkins 2005: 19), a winter depression brought on by the difficulties dealing with the perpetual darkness, brutal winds and freezing temperatures, and being in close quarters with six other fellows, 24/7.

At the end of arctic training, Woody took a brief furlough back to North Dakota to visit his dad on the farm. He then stopped by Detroit, Michigan, to see two friends, who were sisters. Woody's nickname in high school was "guts" because he wasn't tongue-tied around girls.

On the Way to Labrador

After his leave was over, Woody was sent to Presque Isle Army Airfield in Maine. Presque Isle, which means peninsula in French, is about the same longitude as Quebec City, Quebec, and St. John's, Newfoundland. It is an isolated community where Maine juts up to separate Quebec and New Brunswick. The base was a major departure point for U.S. fighter planes during World War II because of its far northeastern location. Along with his six other crew members, Woody waited.

After what seemed like a long time, they were flown into Fort Chimo, Quebec, on the western shore of the Koksoak River which empties into Ungava Bay. The Americans had established a weather station and radio communications centre there, code named Crystal One, in 1941 with the expressed purpose of collecting weather data critical to decisions relating to combat missions in Europe.

An air cargo plane took them into Fort Chimo during a snow storm. When they looked out the window, all they could see was white. The pilot said "Just hang on." They had to land as they didn't have enough fuel to get back to Presque Isle. When Woody could finally see through the snow he said the plane and the runway, rather than being parallel, were about 20 degrees off. In his understated way, Woody commented that the landing was quite a jolt.

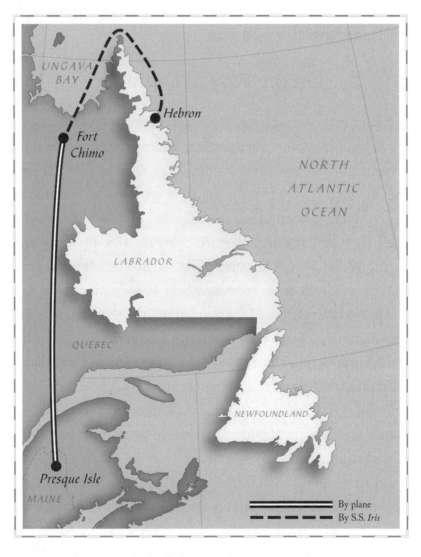

Fig. 14 Woody's itinerary to get to Hebron.
(Illustration: Diane Mongeau)

They stayed in Fort Chimo for a couple of weeks—the final test to see how the group got along. The night before they were to sail for Hebron aboard the *Iris*, an old 325-foot Norwegian luxury liner that had been converted into a transport ship, two of the men in Woody's crew got into a fight and one of them drew a knife. That man was swiftly pulled and another man no one knew, a G.I. named Hank Bradley from Massachusetts, was put in his place as cook.

The next morning the men waited aboard the *Iris*, which sat in the totally dry Koksoak River. The captain of the *Iris* was a Norwegian, but his crew was all from Labrador. When the 35-foot tide came up the river, the *Iris* sailed north out into Ungava Bay, up around the tip of northern Labrador and down the Labrador coast to Hebron. The *Iris* dropped off Woody's team and a year's worth of supplies, picked up the original weathermen and radio crew who had just finished their year in Hebron, and departed for Cape Harrison, an Air Traffic Control radio range station near Goose Bay.

A few hours later, the *Iris* ran into the tail end of a hurricane and the servicemen spent a sleepless night in the heaving seas. The next morning the storm had let up, but the *Iris* hit a rock on the way into the harbour, about a mile off shore. After three hours of waiting for orders to abandon ship, the men were told to keep their life vests on and stay on board, as the captain believed that the vessel was embedded on the rock and had stopped sinking. He decided the safest thing to do would be to wait until daylight. The men spent another sleepless night and by the next morning the seas had calmed enough that a Coast Guard cutter was able to rescue the men and strip the *Iris* of its navigation instruments and radio equipment before it sank (Thompson 1945: 24).

It was the fall of 1943. Woody and the six other young G.I.'s found themselves in an isolated community whose winter temperatures could reach -50 °F, with ferocious winds that often exceeded 155 mph. Their four prefabricated housing and station buildings barely protected them from either. They were charged with taking weather measurements every two hours, around the clock, using delicate equipment that was subject to temperature and wind and relaying those measurements, in code, utilizing a wireless transmitter. There were no doctors, nor dentists. No movie houses or restaurants. Winter brought 18 hours of darkness. They were on their own.

---

[5] Unless otherwise noted, in this chapter, all quotes from Woody Belsheim come from our May 3–5, 2010, conversations.

CHAPTER 3

Hebron, Labrador

WOODY HAD NO REAL IDEA where he was going or what to expect when he got to Hebron. He knew his job was to code and transmit meteorological observations taken by the weathermen: wind speed and direction, temperature, humidity and barometric pressure to Presque Isle, Maine. He had no sense of Hebron's past or present, nor did he have any idea what his life would be like for the next year, other than that he would be in an isolated weather station in the Arctic.

Ancient Inuit Site

Of course, isolation is a relative term. Inuit, Dorset and Thule, as well as Maritime Archaic peoples, had been living at Hebron for centuries. Explorations of numerous Hebron sod houses in the early 1990s, led by Stephen Loring of the Smithsonian Institution, have shown "that considerable cultural materials spanning perhaps 1500 years of Dorset-Thule and

Labrador Inuit occupation are preserved at the Hebron Mission site." (Loring and Arendt 2009: 33–56).

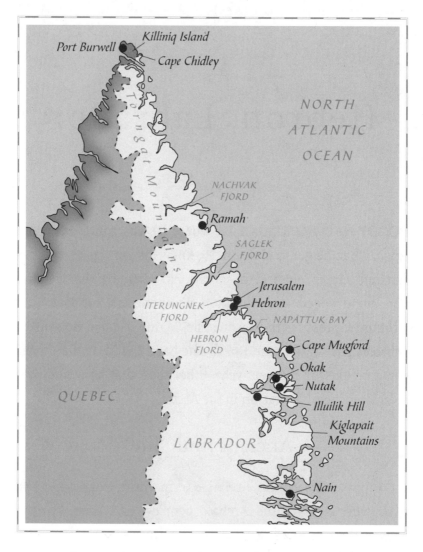

Fig. 15 Northern Labrador place names located north of Nain.
(Illustration: Diane Mongeau)

John Amagoalik, champion of the Inuit homeland Nunavut, wrote: "The land is cold. The land is immense. It is a desert. It is unforgiving. It can be cruel. The land is also home. It sustains life. It breathes. It can bleed. It is part of our mother, the earth. It is beautiful. It nourished our culture. We are part of it as it is part of us. We are one! ... The land shaped our mind and language, our culture, our legends, our philosophy and our view of life." (Amagoalik 2001: 9).

The area around Hebron had long been known by the Inuit as Kangerdluksoak (Periodical Accounts 1871),[6] a good place for seals; seals being essential to the Inuit way of life—for food, clothing, shelter and boats. Earlier in the 19th century, Hebron was a critical Inuit whaling location for both bowhead and white whales. It was also rich in other animals: caribou, fox, fish, Arctic hares, black bears and polar bears. The harbour was sheltered, excellent for kayaks, although the wind was fierce.

Moravian Missions

The Unity of the Brethren, better known today as the Moravians, gave it the name Hebron after the biblical city where Abraham was buried, and David was crowned king. The Hebron mission, founded in 1830, was the Moravian's fourth mission on the Labrador coast, after Nain, Okak and Hopedale. Located about 500 miles south of the Arctic Circle, 25 miles above the tree line and 150 miles north of Nain, Hebron was—after the closing of Killinek and Ramah—now the northern-most mission. Its site was chosen to take the resource pressure off the Okak mission and avoid Hudson's Bay Company posts that were trading with the Inuit farther north (Ibid.).

The Moravians' origins date back to the mid-1400s in Bohemia, now part of the Czech Republic. They followed the reformation teaching of Jan Hus, a university professor who was burned at the stake after being found guilty of heresy in 1415. The Moravians rejected a number of Roman Catholic beliefs, like the idea of purgatory. Hus preached that people should hear the word of God in their own language, that lay people should receive both bread and wine at communion, and that one's soul could be saved by the justification of grace through faith—not by buying indulgences from the church.

The Moravians were persecuted for almost 300 years in their home territories of Bohemia, Moravia and Poland, before finding refuge on Count Nicholas Ludwig von Zinzendorf's estate in Saxony. There, they built the community of Herrnhut, and under Zinzendorf's patronage, committed to taking their version of the gospel to the "poorest and most despised people of the world." By the mid-1770s, the Moravians had missions from Greenland to Guyana (Moravian Church in North America. 2017).

Even though the Moravians lost seven men on their initial exploratory trip to Labrador in 1752, they persisted in their efforts. In 1771, they established their first mission in Nain, after receiving a land grant of 100 000 acres from King George III—who believed that British interests in developing a seasonal Labrador fishing industry, and maintaining peaceful relations with the Inuit, coincided with the Moravians' mission to convert the Inuit to Christianity. However, King George III made sure that the Moravian's land grant did not interfere with the 1670 Royal Charter previously given to the Hudson's Bay Company.

The Moravians would have first heard the name Tuglavina when Jens Haven, the small Inuktitut-speaking Danish missionary who had originally served in Greenland, arrived in Labrador. Mikak, an Inuit woman who had been to London with Sir Hugh Palliser two years earlier, welcomed him. Tuglavina, a powerful shaman, was Mikak's husband (Fitzhugh 1999: 30).

For the next 200 years, the Moravians attempted to insulate the Inuit from the sinful ways of European traders travelling up and down the coast. They conducted services in Inuktitut, and Inuit children were taught to read and write in their own language. It wasn't until 1950, after Labrador had become part of Canada, that the Inuit were permitted to speak English at the mission (Ibid.: 199). As Woody said, he never heard a word of English from the four or five teenage girls who made the weather station their home away from home. He did his best to learn Inuktitut.

For almost 100 years, the sale of Inuit-supplied fur, fish and seal to Europeans served to support the costs of running Hebron's mission. Trading also provided an opportunity for the Moravians to witness to non-Christian Inuit. The dark side of this endeavour was that as Inuit hunted and fished for items to sell, rather than what they needed for survival, they became more and more dependent on the mission for European goods such as flour, sugar, tea and tobacco. By 1926, the Moravians in Labrador could no longer make this arrangement work financially, and it leased all of its stores to the Hudson's Bay Company for 21 years (Kleivan 1966: 128–129). The decision to "relinquish the responsibility for the bodily welfare of its members" and focus on the "spiritual oversight of its flock" (Periodical Accounts 1928: 240) must have been a difficult one for the church.

Hudson's Bay Company

A competitive, adversarial relationship had existed between the Moravians and the Hudson's Bay Company for years. Hudson's Bay Company proponents joked, mistakenly, that HBC stood for Here Before Christ—meaning they had been in Labrador long before the Moravians. With the lease of the mission stores, the HBC became responsible not only for trading furs for supplies, but also for maintenance of the sick and destitute (Ibid.: 129). In exchange for acting in this capacity, the HBC was allowed to import its trade goods to Labrador duty-free (Kleivan 1966: 129).

The Hudson's Bay Company closed its posts in Labrador after 16 years, finding it could no longer make a profit. In 1942, the North Labrador Trading Operations (NLTO), a division of the Department of Natural Resources (a Commission of Government department), took over running the operations. (Brice-Bennett 1994a: xxvi). John Piercy, who had worked for the HBC in Hebron, and his Inuit wife Eugenia, remained at the store. The locals continued to trade their sealskins and furs for food and ammunition. John and Eugenia were still employees at the store when Woody arrived.

Fig. 16 John and Eugenia Piercy. Hebron, Labrador.
(Collection of Elwood Belsheim, 1945)

F. M. Grubb, the missionary at Hebron when the first American contingent of weathermen landed in 1943, didn't think much of the living conditions of the Inuit during World War II: "They live in hovels, with only a few willow twigs and a little seal fat to use as fuel; the large houses take too much heating; parents cooperate and do what they can for their children; when they had the money the people paid their church dues; many coughs and colds in Hebron where overcrowding is mainly the rule; tuberculosis; lack of seals for dog food; laxity in correcting their children therefore they are very headstrong and immoral; morally weak and easily led into immorality, especially the young women; simple folk who live close to nature; know of man's impotence in face of the elements; continually in danger to wrest a livelihood from this bleak land." (Grubb 1943: 41).

Siegfried and Frieda Hettasch

Siegfried Hettasch replaced F. M. Grubb at the Hebron mission in 1944, after the first contingent of Americans had been there about eight months. Hettasch found that "The natives here are pure Eskimos, always with a ready smile on their faces, and quite a number walking about in skin clothes. What struck me as the worst here are the housing conditions. Besides the buildings belonging to the Government or Mission there are about four or five decent houses; the other constructions are made of little scraps of boards from boxes or cardboard, and the bulk built out of grass sods, too small usually for the crowd that lives in it. Cleanliness is almost completely lacking. Hebron is a bleak place; there are no trees. It is a long way to travel to get wood, some 30 miles." (Hettasch 1945: 52). He wrote that many do little to improve their living conditions, finding it easier to seek constant help from the missionary (Ibid.: 53).

Siegfried Hettasch's grandparents had been born in Germany, but had become British subjects, serving as Moravian missionaries in South Africa, where Siegfried's father, Paul, was born in 1873. At the age of eight, Paul was sent to the Moravian boarding school in Germany, transferred to the Moravian Grammar School in Silesia for four years, and then left to work for a tobacco company in Neuweid-on-Rhine. This is where he met his wife, Siegfried's mother, Ellen Mary Koch, daughter of court photographer, Hermann Koch. It was also where he felt called to missionary work in 1894, when he was 21 years old. Paul studied at the missionary training college in Germany for three years before moving to England for a year to learn English, and take medical and surgical training. In 1898, Paul and his wife sailed for Labrador where they began their work in Hopedale. They also served in Okak and Nain, until Paul was named Superintendent of Labrador Missions in 1927. He was replaced in that capacity by F. W. Peacock in 1941, but the Hettasch's continued their mission work in Labrador until his retirement in 1947 (White 2005: 4–5, CNSA).

Siegfried was the youngest of Paul and Ellen's six children. He was born in Nain, Labrador, in early 1915, making him about eight years older than Woody. As was the practice among Moravian missionaries, Siegfried was sent to boarding school in Germany when he was seven years old. At the age of 15 or 16, he left to learn wallpapering, upholstery, carpeting and saddlery trades. Four years later, he went to Fairfield, England, to study at the Moravian Theological College for three years. In addition to theology, he studied English, and also took nine months of medical training, before being ordained as a deacon in the Moravian church in 1938 (Hettasch Fitzgerald 2007).

After sixteen years of being away, Siegfried returned to Labrador where he met and married Frieda Glaser, a Dutch national who had been recruited by Siegfried's older sister Kate to teach school in Nain (Hettasch Fitzgerald 2015).

Fig. 17 Frieda Hettasch with Hebron's school children.
Magdalena Sorglavina is the other teacher seen on the right.
(Collection of the Hettasch Family, ca. 1944,)

Siegfried and Frieda's first child died in Hopedale's 1942 flu epidemic, at the age of nine months (Ibid.). They had two young daughters by the time Woody arrived in 1944. The German, Inuktitut, Dutch and English-speaking Hettasch family were to serve the Moravian mission in Labrador from 1898 to 1980.

Fig. 18 Frieda and Siegfried Hettasch with their children.
Ernie, Ellen and Johanna (Hannie)
(Collection Johanna Hettasch Fitzgerald, late 1940s)

According to the 1945 Newfoundland Population Census, Hebron (Saglek Bay to Narpertokh Bay [Napâttuk Bay]) had 116 people, including the Inuit, the missionary and storekeepers' families, in 23 dwellings (Canadian Dominion Bureau of Statistics, 1949). The majority of Inuit living in Hebron when Woody arrived were originally from farther north—Ramah, Nachvak, Aulatsivik,[7] Saglek and Killinek (Brice-Bennett 1994a; xxiii)—as two-thirds of Hebron's Inuit population, and more than a third of the total Inuit population of Labrador, had died in the 1918 Spanish Flu epidemic that had been carried by a sailor on the Moravian supply ship *Harmony* (Ibid., xxi). These

Northern Inuit were the last to accept Christianity, and were often considered too independent by the missionaries. As their 1939 Periodical Accounts reported, "There is a vast difference between the Hebron and Southern Eskimos. They are made up of Ramah, Nachvak, Killinek, and Aulatsivit [sic] people, and there are no original Hebron people here to act as a foundation on which to work. We have four distinct types of Eskimos, and it is very difficult to get them to pull together." (Harp 1939, 121).

When Hettasch arrived in Hebron he noted that most Inuit families who lived near the mission, did so in sod houses, or *igluvigaks*. These were traditional winter homes dug 4–5 inches into the ground with large stones around the perimeter. The sandy floors were covered with bear or caribou skins, and the rafters were framed by wood or whalebone with sod insulation and seal gut windows (Brice-Bennett 1994a: xvi). As there were no trees near Hebron, sod houses were heated by, and cooking done on, seal oil lamps. Three small wooden frame homes had been built by the Hudson's Bay Company in an attempt to improve Inuit living standards, part of the price the HBC paid for being able to import duty-free goods to the mission posts (Parsons 1929, TRC), but these were so cold in the winter that they were used for storage (Belsheim 2010).

The Newfoundland Ranger Force

Fig. 19 Newfoundland Ranger Force detachment building.
Hebron (194?).
(Collection of *The Rooms*, VA 126-20.1)

The Newfoundland Ranger Force was the third institutional presence in Hebron, in addition to the Moravian mission and the NLTO store, when the Americans arrived. The Newfoundland Commission of Government had established the New-foundland Ranger Force in 1935 to become the government's administrative agents in rural Newfoundland and Labrador, supplementing the urban-based Newfoundland Constabulary (McGrath et al. 2005). The rangers were sent to outposts like Hebron, usually alone, to collect taxes on imported goods, en-force game and criminal laws and to investigate suspicious activities. They also took over the provision of relief assistance from the Hudson's Bay Company. It is likely that the creation of the Newfoundland Ranger Force, and its charge to distribute assistance, were a direct result of the Hebron Inuit "uprising" of 1933–1934 (Evans 2011). Bruce Gillingham, Gerald Hannon, John Howard and Chesley Parsons would probably have served in Hebron as rangers when the Americans were there from 1943 to 1946 (McGrath et al. 2005). They had their own living quar-ters, but spent Saturday nights with the servicemen, sharing beer and stories (Belsheim 2010).

Hebron Bay was large enough for a military seaplane to set down, but only just. The American weather station occupied an acre of land, and was a 10-minute walk from the mission, just across the creek near the cemetery. Inuit homes were on the opposite side of the mission complex. All the servicemen's nec-essary supplies had been flown in with them, so they had little reason to buy anything at the store (Ibid.). It was into this mi-lieu that the Americans arrived.

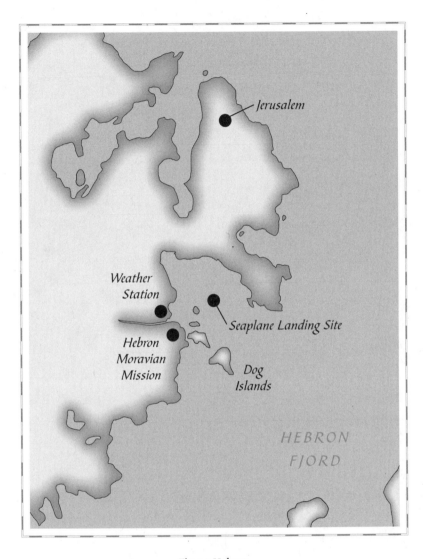

Fig. 20 Hebron.
(Illustration: Diane Mongeau

---

[6] Also spelled Kangikluksoak (Brice-Bennett) and Kangertluksoak (Loring)
[7] Refers to North Aulatsivik Island, between Nachvak Fjord and Cape Chidley, as opposed to South Aulatsivik Island near Nain.

CHAPTER 4

Renatus Tuglavina: Inuit Leader

RENATUS TUGLAVINA HAD NOT BEEN BORN IN HEBRON, but he and his family were living there when the first contingent of American servicemen arrived. Renatus' Inuit name was Kuttaktok. He was born in 1896 at Killinek, on the northern tip of the Labrador Peninsula, which was at the time part of the Northwest Territories. According to Carol Brice-Bennett's genealogical research, Renatus was the son of Tuglavina (who died in 1910) and Tuglavina's third wife Arnatuk (Tabea),[8] who was 22 years old when Renatus was born. Renatus' brother Ananatsiak (Josef) was born in 1902, and a second brother, Kedek (Jonas), was born in 1906. I can't prove it, of course, but I would be willing to bet that the young boy standing off to the left away from the other children in Samuel

King Hutton's photograph of Old Tuglavi's Killinek sod house (Hutton 1912: 40)— featured in his 1912 book *Among the Eskimos of Labrador*—is Kuttaktok (Brice-Bennett 1996). The name Renatus translates from the Latin as "born again," especially after being baptized (Wikipedia 2017c). It was also the middle name of Count Nicholas Ludwig von Zinzendorf's only son, Christian Renatus. Von Zinzendorf, from Dresden, Germany, was instrumental in breathing new life into the Moravian sect in the early 1700s, and in supporting their mission expansion into Labrador.

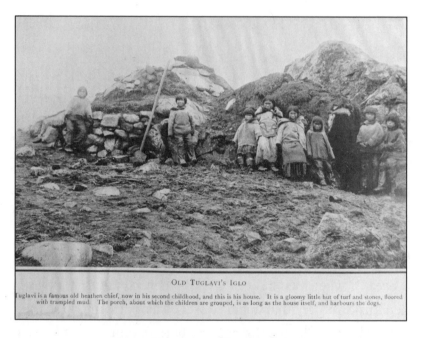

OLD TUGLAVI'S IGLO

Tuglavi is a famous old heathen chief, now in his second childhood, and this is his house. It is a gloomy little hut of turf and stones, floored with trampled mud. The porch, about which the children are grouped, is as long as the house itself, and harbours the dogs.

Fig. 21 Old Tuglavi's sod house in Killinek.
From Samuel King Hutton's 1912 book *Among the Eskimos of Labrador*. (Public domain)

Old Tuglavi and Killinek

The Moravian missionary at Killinek had told Hutton that Kuttaktok's father, Old Tuglavi, was a "famous old heathen chief" who was now in his second childhood. According to Hutton, Old Tuglavi was indulged by the community, given biscuits and allowed to wander in and out of the mission house at will. On one occasion, when it was decided to "keep the old man out of harm's way" by locking the mission door, Tuglavi used a fork with a broken tine to lift the latch. The missionary also told Hutton that Tuglavi had two wives. His first, Pituratsuk, was his lifelong companion. He had married Arnatuk to take care of Pituratsuk and himself in their old age (Hutton 1912: 25–45).

Killiniq was a rocky island and Inuit had been hunting whales, walrus and seals off its shores for hundreds of years. Being so far north, it was the last Moravian mission established in Labrador. Because of the difficulty servicing such a remote location, as well as financial considerations, the mission was closed in 1924, twenty years later. The Hudson's Bay Company, which had established Port Burwell as a trading post on Killiniq Island in August 1916, bought out the Moravians' buildings, outposts, sealing stations, equipment, lands and stock.

Port Burwell's 1921 post journal focused on three areas: The hunt for polar bears, seals, caribou, cod, shark, duck, partridge, fox, ptarmigan, and white whales; the odd visitor, including the polar explorer Knud Rasmussen and Harald Lindow, the Danish Royal Inspector of North Greenland; and the weather: dull, overcast, dark, dirty, cloudy, snow, cold, raw, gale winds, ice, slob, and every now and again, sunshine, clear and calm. Although the journal's Sunday entries usually recorded "this being the Sabbath no work done," there were exceptions as on Sunday, November 6, when the "Eskimaux visited seal nets today getting 10. All hands attended service at the Mission House in the evening." (B.466/a/1: November 6, 1921).

Old Tuglavi died in 1910, when Renatus was 14, but there is no doubt that he and his brothers, all healthy and strong young boys, would have been taught the traditional hunting skills, how to read the weather, and how to survive in the harsh climate that Killinek offered. Pituratsuk was baptized on March 20, 1910 (perhaps after Tuglavi died), and took the name Sabina. Arnatuk was baptized on January 6, 1914, and took the name Tabea. In the Killinek church book she appears to be the wife of Tobias Kairtok. It is quite possible that he was the teacher of Arnatuk's boys (Rollmann 2017).

Renatus was 23 years old when he married Loida Semigak on October 26, 1919. Loida, like Renatus, had been born on the Canadian side of the Labrador Peninsula in 1899. Her Inuit name was Kupa. Her mother was Paniguniak (Harriot), born in 1869. Her father, Anatsiak, passed away when she was five years old. She was the granddaughter of Semigak of Nachvak Fjord who, along with his wife and eight other Inuit, died in the 1905 influenza epidemic north of Ramah (Brice-Bennett 1996a). The Northern Inuit were the last Inuit to accept Christianity. In 1903, the Moravian missionary Gericke visited Semigak, "the heathen chief in the North ... but Semigak remains firm in his determination not to relinquish his heathen beliefs and ways—

nor does the life of most of the native Christians at Ramah tend to influence him in favour of the change. He finds most of them to be but little better than himself, and prefers to remain as he is." (Periodical Accounts 1904: 621).

I first found mention of Renatus in *Igloo Killinek*, by Kenneth C. Butler, who had served in the Royal Canadian Mounted Police (RCMP) at Killinek from 1920 to 1921. I ordered the book on a hunch thinking it possible that, as Killinek was a small settlement, Butler's story might have some information about the Tuglavinas. He mentioned Renatus once: "With the coming of March, the snow month, came news of tragedies in various parts of the country. Our weather at this time was miserable, with drifting snow and cold, strong winds. We were quite surprised when on the first of the month we received four Eskimo visitors, each with a tale of woe. Rene and Renatus came up from Nachvak and reported that the former's wife, Maria, and their child, had burned to death, having used gasoline to start a fire in mistake for kerosene." (Butler 1963).

Fig. 22 Nachvak Fjord.
(Photo: France Rivet, 2016)

Relocating to Hebron

Renatus and Loida's first child, Paulina, was born while they were living near Killinek (Hebron CNSA: 101). They were one of five families that chose to relocate south to Hebron in 1923, after two-thirds of the Hebron Inuit had died of the Spanish Flu during the winter of 1918–1919. It is likely that Renatus' two brothers moved with him. Their second child, Tabea Harriot, named after Renatus and Loida's mothers, was born on April 5, 1926 (Hebron CNSA: 107).

I thought that was all I would learn about Renatus until I began tying up loose ends of my research, reviewing articles and putting interviews in order. Then I ran across a special issue of *Kinatuinamut Ilingajuk*, edited by Peter Evans (Evans 1999), and decided to contact him. Evans was doing his doctoral work at the University of Cambridge in England, but lived in Victoria, British Columbia, where I had visited a week earlier.

I mentioned to Peter that Harriot had told Woody that her father had spent a year in prison for murder, but I could find no record of such an event in the literature. Evans said that Renatus hadn't killed anyone, that he had gone to jail for leading a rebellion against the HBC in the mid-1930s. He encouraged me to get hold of a 1958 book, *Challenger*, written by George Stephen Ritchie when Ritchie was a Captain in the British Royal Navy. Evans also noted that a number of Hudson's Bay Company post journals made mention of Renatus.

These journals record Renatus and his brothers, now called James and Josef rather than Jonas and Josef, in constant motion, travelling up and down the Labrador coast: to Saglek Bay, Iterungnek Bay, Napartok [Napâttuk Bay], Illuilik (the sealing station) and Jerusalem. While the journal writers make disparaging remarks about the Inuit who never leave the Mission, it is clear that Renatus is not one of them. He is most often mentioned hunting and trapping with his brothers or Levi Semigak and bringing in seals and fox fur to trade.

Renatus and his family did come to Hebron for the 1926 Christmas celebration. During that trip, the group ran into heavy winds and drifting snow. According to the Hudson's Bay Company post, all "were more or less frost bitten" and a young girl, Agusta Semigak, froze to death on the way. She "lay in the dead house" while her coffin was being made (B. 418/a/1 HBC: December 16, 1926).

Two weeks later, tragedy struck again, although this time no lives were lost. On Old Christmas, January 6, 1927, "between ten and eleven o'clock one of the mission houses, occupied by Renatus Tuglavina, burned to the ground. The occupants who had retired for the night barely escaped with there [sic] lives, losing all there [sic] personal effects, including guns, etc.; the fire was caused by the occupants neglecting to extinguish a candle before 'turning in'" (Ibid.: January 7, 1927). By the end of February, Renatus had replaced his gear and was headed up to Iterungnek and Saglek Bay.

A few months later, the HBC trader at Port Burwell wrote: "Renatus Tuglavina who carried the mail from Hebron appears to be a very particular and independent sort of person for an Eskimo. Today he refused point blank to carry any mail in return, unless the contents were made known to him, and further, only if he saw fit to do so by his judgment of what it did contain.

Fig. 23 View of St. John's Harbour, Saglek Fjord.
(Photo: France Rivet, 2016)

"Mr. Andrews of Hebron post sent here for a few necessary articles to go by Renatus. If the latter mentioned expects us to crawl to him, he must have been sadly disappointed and no letters nor parcel will therefore be sent by him. We also understand that some of the goods mentioned were for his own benefit.

"Enough dog feed has been supplied to him for his return free of charge. The amount of eight dollars he had on his person, but he complained on it not being enough so we advanced another two dollars making ten in all, being quite ample for to

buy grub, although he did not do so. Buying Mouthorgans, etc."
(B.466/a/6 HBC: April 11, 1927).

In July 1927, Renatus and his family returned to Hebron
from Nain. In September, he packed trout for the HBC. On November 23, he returned to the Hebron post in his motor boat
"which had to be hauled up immediately on arrival here owing
to it having been twisted in a big sea yesterday evening."
(B.418/a/2 HBC: November 23, 1927). With him were Joseph[9]
Tuglavina, Jefta Jararuse, Marcus Lidd and Simon Tuglavina
from Illuilik. They were catching seals in the HBC nets in
Illuilik. Two days later, their boat "fixed," they were off again.

Renatus, along with his brother James, and Martin, Daniel
and Julius Jararuse arrived back at the post on December 23,
1927, "having shot and harpooned between them 100 seals.
Mostly harps and bedlamers [immature seals]. Fox and deer
were very scarce and the going very bad for komatics." (Ibid.:
December 24, 1927). Renatus left for Saglek the day after
Christmas. He returned with his family on January 1, 1928, to
once again celebrate Old Christmas, January 6, at the mission.
Spring of 1928 was tough as foxes, no good for food, but what
the HBC wanted for trade, were not taking the bait either north
or south of the post (Ibid., February 13, 1928).

Living conditions for the Inuit had become critical by 1933-
1934. The worldwide Depression had "gutted markets for cod,
skins, and crafts. In the North, sealing had largely failed in 1933
and only the unexpected appearance of the caribou migration
along the coast—the first time in many years they had taken
this route—saved the day." (Evans 2011: 19).

Adding to their misery, the Hudson's Bay Company had replaced the old mission system whereby Inuit were outfitted against future earnings, with a strictly cash and barter one. Inuit now had to purchase guns, ammunition and other hunting and clothing necessities with wages earned from small jobs or from furs brought in for sale—a Catch-22 if ever there was one. How can you hunt if you can't buy ammunition? How can you buy ammunition if you can't hunt?

The HBC lease of the Hebron store from the Moravians in 1926 was having disastrous effects on the Inuit. Previously, the mission had sold necessities like tea, flour and sugar at a discount while keeping the price of luxury items high. But the HBC calculated a full profit with equal rates on all sale goods, so that the prices of essentials increased considerably. The mission reported that "in the minds of the majority of our people there has been a great deal of dissatisfaction with the new order of things." (Periodical Accounts 1928: 245–246). That dissatisfaction grew as the Depression deepened.

Along with running the Hebron post, the HBC had agreed to provide aid to those in need. Under this arrangement, "considerable pressure was put upon anyone seeking assistance by the fact that the administrator of the aid was, at the same time, the representative of a private business company. The skilled hunter held a more favourable position than others when he sought help in an emergency, or asked for ordinary credit. From a commercial standpoint, he represented a better investment than the man who only seldom brought in a fox skin." (Kleivan 1966: 129).

The HBC now had a monopoly on trade in northern Labrador, so the Inuit had no alternative should the Company pay poorly. Having a good relationship with the HBC manager was almost a prerequisite to obtaining aid when starvation threatened. When the mission was responsible for administering relief, even the Inuit who were on the worst terms with the missionaries would receive a helping hand if there were shortages.

The Inuit often found themselves torn between the mission, which insisted on weeks of church activities during the year, and the HBC manager, who refused to give aid if he considered the Inuit loafing around, i.e., attending church services. Even Woody mentioned his concern that Hettasch expected the men to observe Christmas and Lenten celebrations during the height of fox season.

One HBC trader at the Hebron post wrote, "The weather continues perfect for hunting and when we see so many able-bodied men standing around doing nothing but watch the [mission] band make its sounds we could weep. One fellow saw 16 foxes on a short trip inland for deer to eat on xmas and [instead of shooting the foxes and bringing them in to trade] he came here and got 24 pounds of flour on relief." (B.418/a/3 HBC: December 23, 1941).

Another time, "A native in good standing in the church asked me today to give him enough wood to enable him to stay here till January 6, when the current debauch ends. Naturally, I refused. Especially as he in his zeal for services has been here off and on for the last year and during that time has not brought in one fox." (Ibid.: January 2, 1942).

Hudson's Bay Company Break-Ins

Things came to a head during the winter of 1933–1934 when Renatus, at the age of 37, along with seven other men, broke into the Hudson's Bay Company store at Hebron three times— once in November 1933, when they broke the window of the molasses storeroom, then in January 1934, and again in February 1934 using a key they had made to fit the store's Yale lock. They took clothing and ammunition (Ritchie 1958: 42–50).

This last break-in was recorded in two publications, *Challenger: The life of a Survey Ship* by George Stephen Ritchie, and the journal article *HMS Challenger Wintering Party*, edited by William Glover (Ibid.; Hampson 2005). After reading these accounts, I was curious to find the original source material—the diary of Lieutenant-Commander E. H. B. Baker, of the British Royal Navy. According to Ritchie, Baker brought Renatus back to Nain under house arrest and put him to work for the survey crew, insisting that he continue to hunt for his livelihood. Failing to find an obituary for Ritchie, I turned to the British Telecom phonebook, where I discovered a listing for a Stephen Ritchie living in Scotland, and rang him up. "You'll have to speak louder please, I'm 97 years old and a little hard of hearing" (Ritchie 2011), he said when I told him I was looking for the author of *Challenger*. He thought he could find Baker's diary for me and when I called him back on Monday he had the contact information for Baker's son, Michael, in South Devon, England. Next thing you know, I was on my way to England to read Baker's private journal.

Fig. 24 E. H. B. "Buck" Baker.
(Collection of E. H. B. "Buck" Baker, 1933)

The *Challenger* had just finished mapping the Windward Isles and the Grenadines, when it was instructed to update the hydrographic charts along the Labrador coast. The coastal route was the preferred way of travel as it opened long before the open water route, but it was only sketchily charted. The *Challenger's* mission was to "survey a route inside the islands from Indian Harbour in the south to Cape Chidley in the north." Ice made the *Challenger's* trip to Nain a tricky one. The men soon realized that winter ice, and the shortness of summer, made it all but impossible to complete their work in a timely manner. It was determined that the most efficient way to finish the survey was to leave a crew of men to overwinter in Nain, using dogs and dogsleds rather than boats to chart the harbour and its surroundings.

Baker had been in charge of the survey's winter party for a little over two months when a Mr. Clarke of the Nain HBC post and a Mr. Smith of the Nutak HBC post came to visit him the evening of January 25, 1934. The men chatted for a couple of hours before Clarke said to Baker that Smith wanted to talk with him alone, outside. Baker thought he probably needed to borrow something, paraffin maybe (Baker 1934).

But instead Smith asked Baker "point blank" (Ibid., January 25, 1934) to come to Hebron and "quell the disturbances" (Ibid.). The last HBC trader had left because he couldn't handle the Eskimos and feared that if he didn't give in to their demands, they would have broken down the store. The HBC had replaced him with a 23-year-old Scotsman, David Massie, who had only been with the company for four years. And that was at Rigolet, where there were no Eskimos.

Smith and Clarke asked Baker to go up to Hebron with them and arrest Renatus, "known as being a rascal and the instigator of all the trouble up there." (Ibid.). It would be a 300-mile round trip over snow and ice. Baker told the men he had survey work to do, but when he was finished, he would go up to Hebron to "hang around a day or two and lend moral support to Massie and show the natives that there was someone who had nothing to do with the H.B.C. or the missionaries, within reach." (Ibid.).

That night, however, Baker rethought his original refusal, and decided he would go to Hebron first thing, but he would travel alone—without HBC men—to have a look-see and make sure he wasn't being negligent. Baker was a representative of the British Royal Navy, and he did not want to be considered an extension of the HBC. The Moravian missionary in Nain at the time, F. M. Grubb, offered to go up with Baker, but Baker declined his company, saying it would weaken Grubb's position among the people if it looked like Grubb needed a naval escort (Ibid.). A blizzard didn't permit Baker to travel until a week later.

Baker Puts Renatus Under House Arrest

Baker and his party loaded three komatiks (dog sleds) for the journey over the 1 000-foot-high Kiglapait Mountains. Progress was slow as the snow was soft and once they reached the top of the Kiglapaits they couldn't keep the sleds from outrunning the dogs. It was a difficult and dangerous trip given their lack of knowledge of the area and ability to drive the sleds. In the darkness, they barely avoided collision with a 20-foot boulder, and were up to their chests in snow when they had to right an upturned komatik (Baker 1934, February 1, 1934).

Fig. 25 Eating chocolate on the way to Hebron.
Caption reads: "Doc digging out some chocolate during a 'stand easy' in the 1st
stage—Nain to Tikkeratsuk. (35 m[iles])."
(Collection of E. H. B. "Buck" Baker, 1934)

Fig. 26 At Ama Panagonjak's house.
At the end of stage I, on the way to Hebron.
(Collection of E. H. B. "Buck" Baker, 1934)

Stage III. The Kiglerpait Range from the Northern side. Kurukuluk — Nutak (24m.)

Fig. 27 Kiglapait Mountains.
(Collection of E. H. B. "Buck" Baker, 1934)

The men spent a welcomed night with the Smiths in Nutak. The next day Baker's camera fell off his komatik and when he went back to pick it up he noticed that his kitbag was dripping wet. Unfortunately for him, his large flask of brandy had broken, and in cleaning it up, he cut his thumb which "bled like a stuck pig" (Baker 1934, February 3, 1934). Two of his men were badly frostbitten. Closer to Hebron, they stayed with Willie Tuglavina and his family. "Willie said he was one of the rascals, but at least he was a cheerful one and handled a primus stove like a good 'un." (Baker 1934, February 4, 1934).

After a week of travel, they finally reached their destination, "racing across the sea ice, with their white ensigns flying from each komatik. The Eskimos of the Hebron Settlement had never seen such a sight and, as they watched the arrival, there was much discussion as to who they were and what they had come for, but suspicions were aroused and soon there were few to be seen except Massie, the Hudson's Bay trader." (Ritchie 1958: 47).

Fig. 28 Moravian mission, Hebron.
(Collection of E. H. B. "Buck" Baker, 1934)

Baker and his team stayed in the Hebron mission, which he described as "a great barn of a place, in which the missionary, H.B.C. and store servant all live in different sections. The missionary, Harp, was on leave, the house was as cold as charity, Massie living in one room, using it as a bedroom, dining room and sitting room, to save expenses on fuel I imagine. Dave, the clerk, had the room next to his, but this only had a fire in it just before one turned in at night and did not last long. The office which was on the other side of Massie's room never seemed to have a fire and was a dingy, untidy place which gave one the pip to walk through it, in fact we 3 felt like getting down to it and giving the whole place a thorough cleaning." (Baker 1934, February 4, 1934).

Massie and his wife had a two-month-old baby, "a pretty poor specimen he is, poor little devil, but they go home on furlough in the summer so I hope for his sake that he will get good nourishment when he gets to Scotland." (Ibid.). Massie told Baker that he thought the only way to get peace was to remove Renatus from Hebron as Renatus had been threatened too often and nothing had come of it. Massie also said that Renatus was openly boasting that the law could not touch him (Ibid.).

Baker interviewed a number of Inuit men the next day and all agreed that Renatus was their leader. According to Ritchie, when Baker finally spoke to Renatus, which he did last, he held up his fingers and explained that he (Baker) was third in line after God and King George. Once Renatus knew the level of man he was dealing with, "this thick-set Eskimo looked impressed, his jaw dropped and his attitude at once became more reasonable." (Ritchie 1958: 48). Renatus admitted that it had been his idea to break in through the molasses store window and also to fashion a key for the lock.

Baker said that "Renatus himself told me that he knew he was doing wrong but that he did it in order that something might come of it and that the matter would be investigated over the heads of both Parsons, the district manager and also the H.B.C. post manager." (Baker 1934, February 5, 1934). Baker seemed to agree with Renatus when he wrote, "I must admit that in many ways I think there is something to be said for both sides, and I think the trouble is that the natives of Hebron have been mishandled for a very long time both by the H.B.C. and the missionaries, and it is about time that an inquiry was made into the matter and the whole question thrashed out and squared off." (Ibid.).

Baker told Renatus that he and his family would have to return with him to Nain. Renatus agreed to go, but not until the HBC outfitted him in clothing and ammunition. Later that evening, Renatus had a change of heart and sent another man to tell Baker that he would rather be killed than go to jail. Baker assured him that he wouldn't be imprisoned; that he would be free, but would have to go hunting for his living and work for the survey crew (Ibid.).

Renatus, Loida, and their three children—Paulina (14), Harriot (8) and Josef (2)—travelled south to Nain with Baker on their own komatik. Baker often rode with Renatus on the trip back, at Renatus' suggestion, in order to lighten the load on Baker's komatik and keep the sleds together. At the top of the Kiglapait Mountains, the crew set up tents while Renatus built a snow house for his family (Baker 1934, February 11, 1934).

Ritchie wrote that, "it was a fine clear night, the loveliness of which was accentuated by beautiful aurora with a delicate pink shade on the edge of the usual yellow bands of light; the night was quiet, crisp and still, as the travelers listened for the crackling sound that can sometimes be heard when an aurora is seen from high ground. But not a sound ruffled the immense stillness." (Ritchie 1958: 49–50).

Fig. 29 Returning to Nain with Renatus.
(Collection of E. H. B. "Buck" Baker, 1934)

Fig. 30 Renatus and his family on the way to Nain.
(Collection of E. H. B. "Buck" Baker, 1934)

A week after Baker returned to Nain, he wrote a five-page typed memo to the British Admiralty outlining his trip, and suggesting that a competent higher authority undertake an extensive examination of the relationship between the natives of Hebron and the Hudson's Bay Company, "for it is my opinion that there are faults on both sides and only a thorough investigation can clear up the matter and make for future tranquility, as it appears that the trouble is one of long standing in which no attempt seems to have been made to give the natives a reasonable hearing." (Baker 1934 TRC).

Fig. 31 Renatus building two snow houses.
(Collection of E. H. B. "Buck" Baker, 1934)

The men of the British survey crew admired Renatus' skill and equipment. Thomas Hampson, leading seaman of the survey party, was impressed with Renatus' komatik runners. Able seaman A. J. Marlowe went off with Renatus Tuglavina with a load of gear for the camp. "Renatus doesn't use the ordinary steel runners but sticks to the mud runners of the northern Esquimos. They are beautiful and smooth running." (Hampson 2005: 58). Mud runners were a mixture of mud and moss, applied hot and then smoothed down and iced with water so that the komatik would slide over the snow and ice with little friction.

Tried Aboard the *Kyle* by Abram Kean

Renatus worked for the survey party until early August 1934. After the sea ice had broken up, the S.S. *Kyle* arrived in Nain from St. John's, Newfoundland. The *Kyle* was a familiar sight, having transported supplies and passengers up and down the Labrador coast for about 20 years. Two large policemen, a Sgt. Squibb and another man, came off the ship, arrested Renatus, and took him back on board (The Daily News 1934). Baker arrived shortly thereafter, as he was also leaving on the *Kyle*, bound to St. John's, Newfoundland, and then England.

Abram Kean, the Newfoundland sea captain famous for taking over a million seal pelts, as well as for stranding 78 sealers on the ice to die in the 1914 Newfoundland sealing disaster, was also on board the *Kyle*. Squibb wired the Commission on Justice in St. John's to ask whether Kean, a justice of the peace, might serve as judge in the Renatus matter. Renatus was charged with stealing $190 worth of goods from the HBC. The Commission agreed and authorized Kean to do so (Ibid.).

Fig. 32 S.S. *Kyle* aground, Harbour Grace (NL).
(Photo by Scott Osmond, Hidden Newfoundland).

Baker spoke to Kean on Renatus' behalf before the proceedings and also testified in Renatus' defence, saying that Renatus "had caused the disturbances at Hebron as he thought the Eskimos were being badly treated by the trader there and he wished to cause an investigation of these injustices." (Baker 1934, August 10–16, 1934). Renatus pleaded guilty to the charge, the only evidence against him, and offered that he would never repeat the offence. He had no defence counsel. The Moravian missionary, F. M. Grubb, served as an interpreter and explained to Renatus that Kean had sentenced him to two months of hard labour in the Twillingate jail (Ibid.).[10]

Kean writes in his autobiography that his sentencing of Renatus met with dissatisfaction among many of the passengers on board who, he felt, let their "false sympathy" (Kean 2000: 72) get the better of their judgment. They expressed their belief that Kean did not care about Renatus' family, or who was going to care for them while Renatus served his sentence. But Kean countered that when Renatus was taken to the lock-up, he "had his pockets full of tobacco, cigarettes and money, given to him, no doubt, by the passengers." Kean righteously argued that "the laws and constitution of the English Government are the best in the world because they approach nearest to the laws God has established in our natures." (Ibid.). In Kean's mind, Renatus, by violating the English laws, was violating "the laws of Heaven itself." (Ibid.).

Baker wrote that the trial was "farcical and Gilbertian to a degree and entirely unorthodox, at least according to Adamson, [another passenger who was] a lawyer." (Baker 1934, August 10–16, 1934). When Baker arrived in St. John's the first thing he did was pay a visit to the Commissioner of Justice, William R. Howley, and argue on Renatus' behalf (Ibid., August 17-20, 1934).

In the meantime, Baker's February 1934 memo to his superiors requesting an investigation into the relationship between the Inuit and the Hudson's Bay Company was slowly making its way through British government channels. It was received by the British Admiralty in London and, in June 1934, forwarded to the Secretary of State for the Dominions, who, in turn, forwarded a copy to the Secretary of the Hudson's Bay Company in London, requesting confidentiality. It was then sent to the

Commission of Government in St. John's and ultimately to Commissioner Howley "for his action" (Ibid., February 15, 1935).

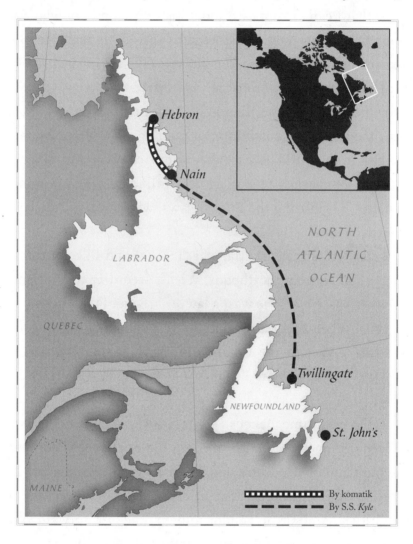

Fig. 33 Renatus' itinerary from Hebron to Twillingate.
(Illustration: Diane Mongeau)

The cover page to the memo to Howley has a hand-written notation on it: "officers now on *Kyle* due Nain on the 9th." Which means that Howley was aware of Baker's concerns prior to Renatus' trial, and before Baker visited him in St. John's (Ibid.), and probably not inclined to show sympathy to a man who had seemingly undercut his authority.

In February 1935, a full year after Baker's original memo to the Admiralty, John Hope Simpson, Commissioner of Natural Resources in the Newfoundland Commission of Government, was visiting the Dominion's Office in London. There he learned that Howley had not replied to the earlier dispatch concerning Baker's memo "in connection with unrest amongst the natives of Hebron, Labrador" that Howley had originally received in July 1934. Simpson requested Howley, "kindly look into this." Howley claimed ignorance, saying that he "was in the dark on this business of replying to dispatches" (Ibid.).

Two months later, D. Murray Anderson, the Chairman of the Newfoundland Commission of Government, wrote to the Dominion Office in London that Renatus Tuglavina had been sentenced to two months of hard labour in Twillingate jail, and was released shortly before his term was over, so that "the last opportunity for the year of sending him to Labrador might be taken" (Ibid., April 16, 1935). Anderson confirmed what Renatus' daughter had told Woody ten years later, that they were "treated to a hero's welcome when they arrived back in Hebron (Belsheim 2010)."

Anderson goes on to suggest that the Newfoundland government find another way to punish Inuit as "transportation to a place in Newfoundland by steamer, and imprisonment in a gaol with adequate dietary, presents itself to them not as a punishment but as an attractive trip to a centre of civilization, the making of which adds to their prestige among their neighbors when they return home." He sidesteps Baker's request to explore the relationship between the Inuit and the Hudson's Bay Company saying that "difficulty is experienced in giving an accurate account." He does say a "distinction must be drawn between those of aboriginal blood and those of British blood." And he goes on to say that nine "young active and intelligent Constables have been detailed to Labrador and will, once they are able to travel, gain a better understanding of the conditions in that area." (Ibid.; Anderson 1935 TRC).

Whether these nine constables would come to different conclusions than Maxwell Button, acting sergeant of the Newfoundland Constabulary, who visited Hebron in 1934 is unknown. Button reported to police headquarters in St. John's: "Regarding living conditions of the Hebron Eskimos there is certainly room for great improvement. Quite a number of them were found to be in a ragged condition but this fault I understand is entirely due to their own improvidence and apparently natural laziness. It is stated that they make practically no effort to better themselves. A large number of them remain on the Post during the entire year depending upon charity for support and it seems that they have no desire to be other than conscientious paupers." (Button 1934 TRC).

The HBC trader at Port Burwell held the same opinion as Button, writing in May 1934: "These natives are very grasping and cunning, happy only when they are getting something for nothing; they will take all the debt they can get and ask for more, then promptly forget about it. The outstanding balances of the past few years show that. Now, however, they get a little debt in the fall, which has to be paid during the winter, and no spring debts are issued. Undoubtedly it will be a year or two before they get used to it, but it certainly won't help matters to be lenient with them in the meantime."

"Previously they were absolutely dependent on us; they couldn't move without receiving food, etc., either as debt or as a gratuity. They knew they had debts but seemed to have no idea of the amount and that a debt is something to be paid. I am glad to say that the outstanding balances for this outfit amount to practically nothing, but as the last few years has been no more than average (maybe a wee bit below average), there was no sense in trying to collect back debts." (B.466/a/13 HBC: May 3, 1934).

The desperate conditions of the Inuit, and the disparaging opinions of the Hudson's Bay Company traders, were little changed during the 1930s. Inuit who lived near the Hebron mission were caught in the increasingly competitive and conflicting interests of the Moravians who desired their souls, and the traders who wanted their fox pelts (Kaplan 1980: 656).[11] The latter had some luck with young William Onalik, who "approached us today to find out if we would feed him on debt while he was learning to be confirmed, our answer was in the negative. We also advised him to ask the mission to feed him but he said no chance of that. Spoke very strongly to him in favour of hunting and he agreed but said that he would be in trouble with the elders and Parson if he went hunting now, by the time he will have known enough to get confirmed the trapping season will be over. He knows this and would rather be hunting but is not man enough to buck the church.

"We had hoped he would continue hunting as he had a good chance to earn enough to buy a rifle which he needs badly and as he is one of our most promising young hunters and as he may have to wait a long time before earning enough again we are very much disappointed over his coming here to learn texts by heart especially as it is unnecessary. Nearly all our young hunters who show promise are here for the same reason ... only two good youngsters continuing to hunt ... this will be severely felt by their families who in most cases are the reason for their coming in. The boys themselves we think would much rather hunt than attend classes all day with a crowd of women.

"Personally I should be willing to give a good deal to have the agreement between us and the mission lifted for a few days. Evidently the mission fears to lose these boys interest in festivals, etc. and is getting a strangle hold on them now for once confirmed he loses half his liberty being answerable to the church for nearly all his actions and being unable to move from post to post without permission." (B.418/a/1-3 HBC, February 24, 1942).

A day later, "Willie Onalik mentioned above came in today and told us that he had reconsidered and was going inland, also another young fellow Wilson Semigak is doing the same, we consider it one of the finest things those boys could do. If we had the Rangers backing and were to use a little tact, we could get nearly all inland but don't wish to go to [sic] far so that we are outside the agreement." (B.418/a/1-3 HBC, February 25, 1942).

HBC traders didn't seem to hold the break-in against Renatus after he returned to Hebron. His ambitious, yet somewhat dangerous (to them), hunting and sealing activities are often recorded in their journals: "Renatus and Joseph who are here to go sealing got their engine fixed yesterday and it broke in another place today, the cylinder head is worn out and they have turned it over to get the best side out even so it is so far gone that its [sic] doubtful if they can go to Illuilik sealing. The only other boat is Simeon Tuglavina's and that is broken in exactly the same way, heaven knows everything in this place has gone wrong in every possible way this summer and fall, there is one hope now not much remains to go wrong." (B.418/a/3 HBC, November 28, 1941).

The next day, there were strong west winds, heavy seas and it was terribly cold, but Renatus had gotten his engine fixed and was hoping to leave for Illuilik as soon as possible. "Everything loose is blowing away, no chance of Renatus getting to Illuilik for some time, saw several pieces of roof from Eskimo houses blowing away, if this gale continues long enough to blow all their houses and church away also we will be more than content, however there is small chance of that." (Ibid., November 30, 1941).

For the next three days, Renatus tried to get up to Illuilik, but the weather refused to cooperate and he had to stay on the post. He was finally able to leave on Tuesday, even though strong west winds, heavy seas and frigid cold had continued. "Renatus left today for sealing station, expect he arrived safely but if his old engine gave out again he will have arrived at his eternal home by morning. He has spent several nights drifting in his boat but would not survive tonight." (Ibid., December 2, 1941). On Wednesday, when all was calm and fine, the post journal noted that "the elements gave Renatus a hard time getting to Illuilik but have apparently relented to let him get his nets out." (Ibid., December 3, 1941).

Throughout December 1941, Joseph and Renatus drifted back and forth from Illuilik with engine trouble. They had fifty seals when they arrived on December 8. On December 12, they returned with their "engine hopelessly broken, when warm weather permits, they will repair it, the cylinder head has three leaks in its jacket and the piston bushing is gone also the rear main bearing." (Ibid., December 12, 1941). On December 28, three days after Christmas, "Renatus, who has not attended the festivals, arrived last night with seven foxes. They saw a good sign inland, traded, and left again. Some of the other lads may get a fox after church if all goes well." (Ibid., December 28, 1941). Renatus was obviously in the good graces of the HBC, which meant he was probably not in the particularly good graces of the mission.

Leonard Budgell Remembers

Leonard Budgell, a lifetime HBC employee, apprentice clerk, and manager at the Hebron post from 1938 until its sale to the government in 1942, remembers Renatus fondly in *Them Days*:

Fig. 34 Leonard Budgell at 18 years old.
(Collection of Kathy Anstett)

"One really stormy day Bill Metcalfe and I had been hunting from the land. When visibility got so bad we couldn't see the seals anyway we decided to go home. It got dark and we were stumbling along on a path we both knew well. Bill was ahead and he suddenly stopped, there was something right across our track. At first I thought we must have gotten off the track but it turned out to be a motor boat hauled up. It had come up a steep slope from the water to where it was. By the boat there were a dozen or so big seals. No one around! It was too dark to see whose boat it was and, anyway, it was so iced up and covered with snow that we wouldn't likely have recognized it even if we had a light. So we carried on home and when we got there John Piercy came in. He said that Renatus and his brothers, James and Joseph, had come in from the north but he wasn't sure how they had come, by boat or on foot.

"We figured no three men could have put that boat where we saw it. It would have taken a dozen or so men. But we still couldn't figure out whose boat it was or how it got there, and as far as John knew no one else had come in. Big mystery!

"The next morning Renatus came in, full of life and happy as usual. And it was their boat we had seen, and three men had put it there. They had a block and tackle but even with that it was a formidable job. They had unloaded their seals and hauled them up, then in the storm and darkness they had hauled the boat out over the ice-covered rocks and up on the path where it would be safe.

"When the weather cleared they got ready to go back. They brought their seals in to Hebron to be left for use during the winter. Bill, John and I went back to help them get the boat in the water again. We were really not necessary. They turned the boat around on the ice where she lay, pointed her towards the water, which was hardly water anymore just a thick mixture of slob, got the engine ready and once she hit the slope she slid like a *komatik* on the ice and, with a little juggling to protect the propeller and rudder, they were soon afloat again. Conditions were so bad I would never have gone out in a boat but away they went. The water was so thick with snow that I expected to see them bogged down. They were pretty slow but finally made it out of the harbour and into clearer water though there was a big sea heaving in.

"A couple of days later everything was frozen over as far as you could see. I was worried about Renatus and his crew but everyone said that they would make it. Sure enough, James and Joseph arrived by dog team. Yes, they got home okay, and they had pulled the boat out for the winter at their camp. Joseph seemed surprised that I was at all concerned. They had planned to bring a load of seals in for the winter. They did just that and had gone home again. I could see he was wondering why this white man thought there was anything out of the ordinary about it at all.

"It took a bit more to make me realize just how self-reliant and tough these men were. I got the lesson another fall. The seal fishery was over; all the boats were hauled out and a few calm days and nights provided an ideal ice front for hunting right off Hebron. The ice stretched about three miles off shore, smooth as glass and there were dozens of ring seals along the outer edge. Everyone knew that the first off-shore wind would likely take this ideal sheet of ice away and everyone was anxious to get as many seals and, perhaps, walrus and white whales as he could while the going was good.

"I had a good team of dogs and I followed Renatus and his brothers out to the floe edge one fine morning. We were more than usually successful and I soon had a load of seals to take back. At the same time, I noticed that the wind had come off-shore and was blowing quite strongly. I had no desire to go sailing out to sea so I called Renatus' attention to the wind and I headed for the land. Looking back, I could see the other teams following me but they had left their seals on the ice behind them.

"When I got to where the floe ice met the solid bay ice there was a wide crack, rapidly getting wider. However, I found a place to cross and got my dogs and *komatik* on safe ice. The three other teams soon arrived but the crack was much too wide for them to cross. I shouted that I would go back to Hebron, about six miles away, and get boats and men and be back as soon as possible. The three men didn't seem too concerned, all three of them sitting comfortably on their *komatiks* smoking their pipes.

"I went back to Hebron as fast as I could. I even dumped my seals to make the *komatik* lighter. The first snow house I passed was Renatus'. I ducked in and found his wife sitting there cleaning a fox. I told her that Renatus and his brothers were on drifting ice and that I would arrange to get men and boats and go back to rescue them. She looked at me but didn't say much. I guess I expected her to start wailing but she just kept on cleaning her fox.

"There were a few men around but no one was interested in digging out boats or getting ready to go anywhere. One old man, Gustav, smiled at me when I spoke to him. He said not to worry about Renatus.

"Bill Metcalfe and John Piercy had gone in another direction and I had to wait until they got back to get any sense into what was going on. No one seemed to care. When Bill and John arrived I told them and they laughed, said that was an old game of Renatus'. It's always good hunting on drifting ice. The wind might blow off-shore for a while but it always turns around and people get back to the land. Hebron people had been known to drift as far south as Nain.

"I decided to quit worrying but couldn't help wondering about those three men, especially on cold, stormy nights. Then one day three teams were seen coming from south. Someone said casually that it was likely Renatus, James and Joseph. And it was, fat and happy with a number of foxes and *muktuk* [frozen whale skin and blubber, usually eaten raw] enough for all the village to have a feast. They had gotten ashore down near Cape Mugford. (25–30 miles south!) There was a good sign of foxes there. They had collected lots of meat and fat on their drift and had come to pick up their families to go back to their caches and spend the winter.

"I got wise, I quit worrying about Renatus and his crew. The north Labrador was not a cold inhospitable place to them, it was home. They knew how to deal with it and it never got tough enough to beat them.

"They weren't the only ones like that. The whole gang was tough and tireless, it was perhaps that Renatus and his brothers were a bit more visible. They stood out.

"They were a happy people at Hebron. I'd been told that they were a tough gang but it couldn't have been further from the truth. They were independent and didn't like to be ordered around, but, if one minded his own business, they were a great bunch to work with." (Budgell 1990: 54–57).

---

[8] Arnatuk is also sometimes spelled Arnatok. Old Tuglavi's second wife had died when he married Arnatuk. Arnatuk appears as the wife of Tobias Kairtok in the Killinek Church Book while her children retain the Tuglavina name. It is likely that the missionaries didn't sanction or recognize her earlier relationship with Old Tuglavi. Pituratsuk, who took the name Sabina upon baptism, is the only wife listed in the Killinek Church Book for Old Tuglavi.

[9] The HBC journals always spelled Josef's name the English way, Joseph, rather than the original German way, Josef.

[10] There is a discrepancy in reports of Renatus' sentence. Kean and Baker both say Renatus was sentenced to two months of hard labour at the Twillingate jail, while *The Daily News* reported that he had to spend two months of hard labour at the Twillingate hospital. It was later confirmed that he was sentenced to jail.

[11] This ongoing conflict between the Moravians and the HBC for the Inuit's loyalty began in the 1800s and was responsible for the "breakdown of economic and social ties within and between Eskimo communities."

CHAPTER 5

An American G.I. in Hebron: 1944–1945[12]

BY THE TIME WOODY AND HIS TEAM ARRIVED IN HEBRON, the Moravians had been there for just over 100 years, or five to six generations. Renatus and his family had been there for twenty years. The Newfoundland Rangers had been there less than ten years. The Labrador government store was only two years old, having taken over from the Hudson's Bay Company in 1942. This was the second contingent of American weathermen and radio operators to arrive.

Woody was 22 years old. His easy confidence and curiosity served him well. The insight that came with the vision of Jesus and the trap door, as well as his avoiding certain death on three earlier occasions, gave him a sense of being protected. Having grown up in an isolated farming community, he was used to being alone. He had lived most of his life without "conveniences."

Getting Organized

The coldest recorded temperature in Hebron during Woody's time was -30 °F (-34 °C), a common winter occurance in North Dakota. The winds, however, were a different thing and they twice measured over 155 mph (250 km/h), pegging their anemometer. The ferocious gusts caused their oil heaters to backfire when it hit about 75 mph (120 km/h), so after having a bad fire scare, they decided that they would simply shut off all their heaters, go to bed, cover up and wait it out, which they did on more than one occasion.

The men were housed in flimsy wooden barracks that surprised the Inuit as they thought that "we Americans had the best of everything and they couldn't for the life of them understand why we had the worst housing!" (Madsen 1946).

Fig. 35 Secret American weather station, Hebron.
(Collection of Elwood Belsheim, 1944)

Their four buildings were called stout houses, prefabricated structures put up by the U.S. military when it needed quick temporary accommodations. They were made of four-foot wood composition sheets. Each consisted of two half-inch-thick panels with three-quarter-inch wood spacers between the panels for insulation. The buildings had pitched roofs, and every four feet, steel cables were slung overtop and anchored to the bedrock to ensure that they wouldn't be blown away.

Woody estimated that the living quarters for the seven men was approximately 16 feet x 48 feet, or 768 square feet. Unfortunately, both of its doors faced north, where the wind and snow came from. They were constantly shovelling snow, both inside the house where it came through the cracks, and outside in order to keep a path clear to their work area. They eventually solved the problem by digging snow blocks, like what one would do when building an igloo, and using the blocks to create a walled tunnel on the north and east sides of their house, so that they could enter from the south. The operations building held the radio and weather equipment plus a large pantry. Two other buildings housed their four generators, and were used for miscellaneous storage.

The U.S. Army had earlier dropped off their food and drink supplies, but they soon realized that the crew ahead of them had eaten much of their meat, and drunk half the beer. The Inuit provided the men with seal meat, although none of them particularly liked it. Woody ate the liver, which he said had a much stronger taste than calf liver. They fished for cod, salmon and flounder when they could, and enjoyed them deep-fried in butter. They still had 26 cases of beer to split between the seven of them, and they made every Saturday night beer night, inviting the Newfoundland Ranger to join them for a few.

The men were allowed to have contact with only one outside person for the year they spent in Hebron. Woody chose his dad. He could send one coded, 25-word message a month, but could not give any indication of where he was. Somewhere along the way, their messages were decoded and relayed by post. The men were told to designate someone else to receive their paychecks while they were in Labrador, so Woody sent his to his dad, who was still farming in North Dakota. He figured he would have a little nest egg when he got out of the service as there was no need for money in Hebron. Unfortunately, when he went home to collect it, he found that every dime had been spent. His dad just told him, "That money's gone!"

A military plane flew over, and dropped mail to them every three months. The first time this happened was on a windy day, and the two parachutes of parcels ended up in Hebron Bay. Luckily for them, the Inuit were able to retrieve the drop and they salvaged some of the mail. Woody said that he often saw Inuit women with dresses made out of nylon parachute material. Only once during their stay did a plane land on the ice to pick up mail.

The first day they arrived, the men found their living room filled with mothers and their daughters. While they were exploring their new surroundings, they discovered a record player and phonograph albums, so they put on some music. Very soon, all the women were dancing, bouncing up and down. And while they enjoyed the music, the main reason they were there was to measure the men's feet. The men took off their shoes, and the women drew a pattern of their feet. They soon returned with two pairs of sealskin kamiks for each of them. One pair was covered with fur for Sunday wear, for good. Woody never wore the good ones, but he used the untanned, but well-chewed, work kamiks every day until the day he left. The waterproof kamiks fit him like a sock. They were tied just below the knee, and although they often felt damp, they weren't; it was the heat from his body inside the kamiks that kept him warm and his feet were never cold. The women also made each of the men a sealskin parka.

Fig. 36 Hebron settlement (left). U.S. weather station (right).
(Collection of Elwood Belsheim, 1945)

Woody was a bit overwhelmed by all the people who had come out to greet them. There was an odour very new to him, but as soon as he began wearing his sealskin boots and parka, he realized that it came from the clothes they wore, not from the Inuit themselves. Soon, they all smelled the same. Woody said he "found out pretty quickly that they were human beings too and I treated them with respect, never a thought to criticize them about their way of life." (Belsheim 2010).

The mothers came over often, and about four or five teenage girls spent as much time with the servicemen, listening to music and sitting in their comfortable chairs, as they spent in their own homes. The girls never spoke a word of English, so Woody borrowed a 2 500-word Inuit dictionary from Hettasch and began learning "a bit of Eskimo" (Ibid.). Renatus' niece, Hulda Tuglavina, was hired to help the cook do dishes and general cleaning. She was paid with gallon cans of food.

Fig. 37 Inside the weather station living quarters.
(Collection of Elwood Belsheim, 1945)

Woody said it wasn't unusual to see a man's face at the window when it was dark outside, checking them out. The Americans had much more food than they could ever use, and they handed it out freely. Yet, the Inuit never "asked us for things like they did the ranger and Hettasch" (Ibid.).

The weather station was just beyond the Moravian cemetery and near a number of traditional Inuit graves, human remains that had been covered with rocks. As there was little vegetation at Hebron, Woody said the missionary had the Inuit bring in dirt to make the cemetery, which was only about two feet deep. When it was filled, they hauled in another two feet of dirt. When he was there, they were on their third layer. Woody explored the graveyard and noticed that many deaths were the result of childbirth, both moms and babies.

It took some time to get their radio equipment in working order. When they arrived in Hebron, they found two of their four generators didn't work at all, and the other two didn't work very well. They needed two in good running order to operate the station. Luckily for them the cook they took on at Fort Chimo, Hank, was not only an excellent cook, but also an experienced mechanic. He tore one of the generators apart for parts and got two others "purring like kittens" (Ibid.) and the third one ready, if needed, which it never was.

They were also lucky that the radio maintenance man had been a ham radio operator for years, and immediately spotted several problems with their system. It took him about a week to rebuild the entire system. There was never a problem with the radio after that. Woody said the maintenance man "had nothing to do for the rest of the year and, I swear, spent 16 hours a day sleeping." (Ibid.).

Woody's best friend in Hebron seems to have been the mechanically inclined cook, Hank Bradley. They had enough time on their hands to explore their surroundings, and indulge their curiosity. Even though Hank hadn't trained with the team in Colorado, the two of them took their dog team, consisting of 8–10 dogs and a borrowed dog sled, and went south looking for timber, a 15–20-mile trip. Their plan was to build a dock on top of the ice, using the timber and their empty oil drums, so that when summer came, they would have a place to tie up their old WWI-era barge and their 22-foot sponson-equipped canoe.

Fig. 38 G.I.'s skiing in skivvies and sealskin boots, Hebron.
Woody is on the far left.
(Collection of Elwood Belsheim, 1945)

They saw fresh bear tracks, but that didn't stop them from cutting down and loading four 20-foot trees on the dog sled. While they had had training in driving dog sleds in Colorado, it wasn't nearly enough, as they found they couldn't control the loaded sled's downhill movement or speed on the return trip. As

Woody said "the Eskimos are in front of the sled and they know how to whip it back and forth like skis to control the speed, but we couldn't do that, so our sled was going faster than the dogs could run, and we got to the bottom and all the dogs were dragging along behind us." (Ibid.). The dock served them well until a violent storm tore it up, the day before they left.

The sponson floatation strips on the canoe provided some stability, but not enough to turn it safely into a sailboat, which they tried to do by putting a deep rudder at the stern and a high mast and canvas sail towards the bow. Woody was out in this contraption alone one day when the wind came up. He lost control and was blown across the bay. Luckily for him, he caught the tail end of one of the Dog Islands. If he had gone past that point, he would have been out in the Atlantic, and hard pressed to escape death a fourth time.

Woody was amazed that when the ocean ice first froze in the fall, when it was only an inch thick and still soft, the whole village went out sliding. The Inuit didn't pick their feet up and walk naturally, but rather slid forward using their weight to push the ice down, forming a hump in front of them the entire time. The ice was moving up and down, and the villagers were walking uphill on it. It wasn't something Woody dared try, but he said they knew exactly what they were doing.

When the ice finally broke up in early summer, the men watched the Inuit move all their sled dogs to the Dog Islands where two families stayed with them in a tent until fall. Every day, the Inuit shot a seal, and while they were skinning it, their dogs formed a circle about 30 feet away. When they had finished, they stood up, each grabbed a pole, and started beating the dogs to keep them from tearing each other apart in a frantic rush for the meat.

Woody had never done a lot of hunting or fishing, but he soon learned to catch fish by "jiggin." The men chose their spot by watching the whales, which were always around. When they broke water three times and dived, that's where they dropped their line. They didn't have rods, but tied a lead weight that had three hooks to a heavy cord, then dropped the weight to the bottom, and gave it quick jerks. In no time at all, they had hooked one and sometimes two fish.

One afternoon, they saw schools of salmon swimming into the ocean cove where they dumped their trash. They had a fishing net in the storage shack, so they put it across the cove. Once the tide was out they started pulling out salmon with the help of a couple of the Inuit men. By the time the water got so low that the fish stopped swimming into the cove, they had two barrels of salmon. The Inuit cleaned them and hung them on drying racks. Woody said the "big winners were the kids, who loved fish eyes! I never ate one, but to them it must have been like finding a large jug of jelly beans." (Ibid.).

Woody also went up to a small waterfall above Hebron to watch the Inuit catch spawning salmon. The Inuit moved rocks in a way so that some of the water at the bottom of the waterfall was caught by the rocks, and ran off onto dry land instead of back into the stream. The Inuit beat the waterfalls with poles, knocking the fish back downstream. Some of the salmon fell back into the main stream, but a lot of them fell into the one that ran onto dry land, where the Inuit could pick them up.

Fig. 39 Hebron, the Dog Islands and Hebron Bay.
Seen from the hill behind the weather station.
(Photo: France Rivet, 2009)

Fig. 40 Hebron and the Dog Islands seen from Hebron Bay.
(Photo: France Rivet, 2016)

Under the Wing of Renatus Tuglavina

After a few months, Woody became close with Renatus Tuglavina and his family, especially Renatus' daughter Harriot. Renatus had learned English during the seven months he had spent with the survey crew in Nain, and the two in the Twillingate jail, which made him easy to visit with.

Renatus took Woody under his wing. They shared many adventures, including a caribou-hunting trip where Woody ate raw, but frozen meat. The men cut off a large chunk of meat for Woody with their big hunting knives, and Woody took out his little pocketknife, sliced a smaller piece, and stuck it into his mouth. He didn't dare try to eat the way Renatus did. He was over at Renatus' house once when Renatus had just returned from hunting. Harriot had fixed her dad a massive dinner, a pyramided plate of meat over a foot wide. Renatus picked up a hunk of meat, stuck it in his mouth, and then cut it off right at his lips. "All he had was a knife to eat with and he kept it sharp!" (Ibid.). Woody was sure he would chop off a piece of his nose if he had tried it!

Most of the hunters took the sights off their rifles, preferring to sight straight down the barrel. According to Woody, they never missed, even when they were in a boat. "One shot and they got a seal." (Ibid.). Woody was given a gun so he could claim a seal, but rather than shoot it in the neck, so it would remain above water, he missed and instead hit it in the head. The seal sank. Woody described the way the hunters would bring in the wounded seal by grabbing the seal's lip with their own teeth, bobbing it up and down in the water to get some momentum, and at just the right time, flip it over their head into the boat. He said they were excellent hunters, never wasting a bullet, nor killing what they didn't need. He was also taken with the fact that when somebody "catches a seal or something, the whole community eats, They share everything. No this is mine; this is yours stuff. None of that. They are good people, really." (Ibid.).

It was a big deal to be the first boat to reach Nain when the ice broke up in the spring. Among the Inuit, Renatus had the largest boat in Hebron, about 16 feet long with a 10-foot beam, and an inboard one-cylinder motor that rode the waves well. He invited Woody and one of the weathermen to join him for the 150-mile trip to Nain. His entire family was along as were two or three young Inuit men. As soon as they left the bay, there was more ice than water. They stayed near the shore, and twice while heading south, they found themselves completely surrounded by ice. Renatus jumped out of the boat, walked to shore, climbed high enough to get a picture of the area, and decided where to break through. When he returned to the boat, he gunned the motor and hit the ice going full speed, 3–4 knots. When the ice cracked, everyone jumped out, half on each side, with their feet on the ice and hands on the gunwale. They pushed hard enough to open a gap for them to move through. One of the things they brought back to Hebron was used chewing gum which was available in Nain, but not in Hebron. The Nain Inuit didn't throw the gum away when they had finished. They wadded it up until it was about the size of a large cookie, and traded it to the Hebron Inuit. Woody was unclear on what use the Hebron Inuit made of it.

On the return trip from Nain, Renatus' boat caught up to the storekeeper's, which was about the same size, but much nicer, and it became a race that Renatus won. Woody said Renatus "was an expert seaman who knew how to take advantage of the ocean swells to make his boat go downhill more than others." (Ibid.). The only comment Woody ever made about Renatus' sod house was that he guessed that "having a good boat for sealing and fishing was more important to him than having a better house for his family." (Ibid.).

One day Woody walked into Renatus' house when they were having a beer bust. He said he didn't know how they got the yeast to make it as the "ranger watched them like a hawk," but they were intoxicated. Renatus offered him a bottle. "It looked like beer and smelled like beer, but when I held it up to the light, I could see that it was loaded with caribou hair, so I handed it back to Renatus with a ouk nakomik (no, thank you)." (Ibid.), said Woody. And while Woody had no idea how the Inuit got the yeast to make the beer, it is clear in a letter from the British Mission Board of the Moravian Church, and addressed to Br. F. W. Peacock, that they believed the American soldiers were instrumental in providing the necessities for manufacturing of "moonshine."[13]

Friendship with Harriot Tuglavina

Four of the seven Americans had what Woody referred to as "steadies"—girlfriends whose mothers had paired them up with the servicemen. It wasn't something that happened right away. As Woody said "We'd been there quite a while before things developed; the mothers would come in and you knew what they were saying; they wanted us to get together with their daughters, and they were serious about it." (Ibid.).

Fig. 41 Woody, Clara Jararuse and Harriot Tuglavina.
(Collection of Elwood Belsheim, 1945)

Hettasch visited with the Americans the first day they arrived. He told them that there was no venereal disease in Hebron and he wanted to be sure it stayed that way. "Maybe that was his way of saying *Leave the girls alone*, but to us it meant *They are safe*." (Ibid.). That, along with the 200 condoms in their supply closet, and the mothers' encouragement, seemed like a green light to the servicemen.

Perhaps it started with their bathtub, which was set up in the kitchen. Since they carried water from quite a distance, and then heated it on the stove, they each had one day a week to bathe. Woody's was Saturday. The tub's location wasn't exactly a private place. One evening while he was enjoying his bath, Harriot walked in and offered to scrub his back. He considered it a great treat and soon all the G.I.'s were having their backs scrubbed.

Harriot, Renatus' second daughter, became Woody's steady. Woody showed me photographs of the two of them that he had saved for 65 years. He also had pictures of other G.I.'s in the unit, a few of the Inuit girls, their living quarters and the Hebron landscape.

Woody had always liked girls, and had had many girlfriends. But as a young man of 22, Harriot was his first intimate experience. It was wartime, he was in a foreign country away from all that he knew and loved and her warmth and companionship was a godsend. It kept him, as he said later, sane. Harriot had a child, a healthy baby boy she named Josef Kefas Andreas Tuglavina, in May 1945, about five months after their first encounter so Woody knew he was not the father. Harriot wasn't able to breastfeed Josef, so other young mothers helped with their own milk. It was not unusual for Inuit women to have one or two children before they were married, so this did not reflect poorly on Harriot.

Fig. 42 Woody and Harriot Tuglavina, Hebron.
(Collection of Elwood Belsheim, 1945)

Woody had become part of Renatus' family by this time, so when Harriot's older sister, Paulina, had her first child, Harriot fetched Woody insisting he come at once to see the baby. It was a dark winter afternoon when they walked into the house. Paulina's husband was sitting on their bed holding the newborn, but Paulina was nowhere to be found. Ten minutes later, she returned carrying two buckets of water. The spring where they all got their water was a bit of a hike, and Woody was flabbergasted, but said "I guess fetching water was her job." (Ibid.).

Having a mechanical mind, Woody was fascinated with how the Inuit created a cradle for their babies by hanging two ropes, salvaged from the parachutes, from the roof of their sod houses. They spread the ropes apart, using sticks about 18 inches long. Then they took a blanket or skin and put it underneath the ropes, turned it over and over, and lay the baby in it; nothing was anchored down, nothing was fastened, but the weight of the child kept it from falling out.

Woody was never one to sit still. When he noticed that the girls were always combing their hair with their fingers, he made them each a comb from sheets of plastic they had in their storage shed, cutting as many tines into the plastic as he could. He once took an aluminum nut, polished it up and scoured the insides so it was smooth and fit his finger. Then he carved a W in the front and inlaid it with ivory. He gave the ring to Harriot. Another time, he built kitchen cabinets for the cook, and later, for their 60 record albums, which he then catalogued and numbered alphabetically. The men even made skis and tried to use them with their sealskin boots!

Woody credits Renatus and Harriot's friendship for keeping him sane during his year in Hebron. One of the other crewmen didn't fare as well, and got a kick out of buying gunpowder from the government store to make pipe bombs. The last bomb he made used a two-inch pipe about eight feet long. He and Woody walked some 30 feet away to blow it up, but Woody said it didn't amount to much. On the other hand, the guy went "kind of nutty up there. He liked to take a gun up into the hills and shoot at stuff; he had a heyday when the lemmings migrated. But when he started shooting at us, we had to put all our ammunition under lock and key so he couldn't get his hands on it anymore." (Ibid.).

Fig. 43 Moravian mission, Hebron.
(Collection of Elwood Belsheim, 1945)

There was little love lost between the American servicemen and the Moravian missionary. The G.I.'s didn't attend regular services, although at Christmas, Woody asked whether he might bring bags of treats for the children, and Hettasch agreed. But Hettasch was unhappy that the girls spent so much time with the Americans, and strongly disapproved of their relations. He wrote in the 1945 Periodical Accounts, "the natives here are morally weak and are easily led into temptation ... then too some of our people took to getting themselves drunk and caused lots of trouble ... but how can the spiritual life make any progress ... while one man tries to preach the message of Salvation, other white men undermine the very foothold of our people's faith in Christ. It will take a long time to build up what has been torn down in so short a time." (Ibid.).

The Americans never trusted the missionary and felt he was hiding something from them, because he wouldn't allow them into the room where he kept his radio equipment. The mission building had a lot of antennas on the roof, and even though one of the crew tried repeatedly to get into the office to listen to the radio, he was refused.

Hettasch told the men that the Inuit were Christians, but it didn't take Woody long to doubt him when he found the Inuit were fearful of northern lights. Woody also said every married man had a sidekick—someone's wife who would be sexually available to him when his own had her period—so he wasn't convinced that the Inuit totally accepted Christian morality.

And yet, when Woody's tooth began to hurt, Hettasch told him to "come on over and I'll fix it." (Ibid.). So, Woody crossed the stream to the mission, sat in a chair and Hettasch took out his tools, ground out the cavity, put in a filling and sent him on his way. One of the first things the U.S. Army did when the men got back to the States, was to give everyone a thorough medical examination. The dentist who took X-rays of Woody's tooth said Hettasch had done a good job. "He was a master of all trades," (Ibid.) mused Woody, expressing one craftsman's admiration for another.

Saying Goodbye

On August 30, 1945, it was time for Woody to say goodbye. Germany had surrendered to the Allies on May 7, 1945, and Japan would on September 2, 1945. World War II was over. Even so, a plane was bringing a third cohort of weathermen and radiomen to Hebron. Woody was ordered to pack up all his belongings, including the kayak model Renatus had made for him, and be ready to meet the plane by noon. Harriot followed Woody around all morning, helping him pack and chewing the sealskin kamiks he had worn all year for the last time. He gave her his two pillows, his high school graduation ring and the two one-dollar bills that had been in his wallet for a year. He tried to explain to her that, being in the military, he had no choice but to go. When the plane arrived, the servicemen, Harriot, her baby Josef and several other Inuit loaded onto the old barge and went out to meet it. Woody said he stood by Harriot until it came time for him to board. "As I entered the plane, I turned and gave her one last look. It was over. I wasn't a hunter. I wasn't a sealer. It was sad, but it had to happen." (Ibid.).

The war was over. While Woody had been suspicious of the Moravian missionaries, he had never found any evidence that they were German sympathizers. I suspect Hettasch kept the Americans out of his office simply because in his mind they had no right to be there. That and his complete disapproval of the servicemen's relationships with the young Inuit women, and his belief that the Americans had provided the Inuit the necessary ingredients to make alcohol (primarily yeast), would have been enough to put a severe strain on their relationship. Sex and alcohol usage among the Inuit had been issues for the missionaries since they arrived in Labrador, and there was a strong feeling that these servicemen had set their efforts back significantly. When the last cohort of Americans left Hebron in February 1946, Hettasch wrote, "... the men of the local U.S. Weatherbase were taken out by plane, and ever since the place has been deserted. Hebron seems to have become once again the quiet and isolated Mission Station in the North." (Hettasch 1947: 40).

In addition, Superintendent of Missions in Labrador, F. W. Peacock, wrote, "The war news continues to be good and I hope that we shall soon finish the Austrian painter off. His latest pilotless aircraft, or, as they call them now, bombs, are a nasty piece of work intended no doubt to terrorize civilian populations. I couldn't get the news this morning, I am anxious to hear about the naval battle in the Pacific." (Peacock 1944, LAC).

Hettasch's brother-in-law, who lived in Holland—which was under German occupation during the war—wrote: "... a lot has changed. Sunday night October 29 at 6:30 p.m. the first Canadians walked into the village and we were FREE ... Great joy and terrific relief came over us, as if something fell off us. Walking and standing we ate some sandwiches. By half past 7 we heard a car come into the village. We ran out and there was the first jeep with one, yes, one Canadian. Beret on his head, wearing a light raincoat, but a shiny pistol in his hand. A broad shouldered young fellow as fresh as a chicken. Not long after came the rest. One tank after the other. And then we all jabbered and helped to find quarters for the men. That night I had four English cigarettes, boy did they taste good!" (Glaser 1945, CNSA).

Hettasch himself wrote in the June 1946 *Periodical Accounts*: "On May 8th, when peace was announced over the European battlefield, we too tried as best we could to join in the celebrations. Several members of our Brass Band seated themselves on the church roof and started playing 'God save the King' and 'Now thank we all our God,' and many other tunes.

Fig. 44 Hebron Mission Band.
(Collection of Elwood Belsheim, 1945)

"We had a fine sunny day which was of great help, especially in the afternoon, when we listened to the King's message to his people. The window was opened and the loudspeaker placed on the windowsill. Even though most of our people cannot understand English, they were fascinated just to hear their King's voice speaking to them. In the evening, we gathered in church and joined in a thanksgiving service of prayer. Hymns were chosen so that both in English and Eskimo we could sing them to the same tunes. This enabled our American neighbors and our ranger and storekeeper to join in with us. Late in the evening we rung out the festive day with both bells." (Hettasch 1946: 46).[14]

Fig. 45 Hebron Mission Band in winter.
(Collection of Elwood Belsheim, 1945)

Sixty-five years later, sitting in his beautiful home on the Sacramento River, Woody told me, "I can honestly say that, ever since leaving Hebron, I've thought of Harriot often, and have always hoped she would marry a guy who truly loved her and gave her a good life." (Belsheim 2010).

Fig. 46 Woody Belsheim in sealskin coat.
(Collection of Elwood Belsheim, 1945)

Fig. 47 Souvenirs from the Far North.
Caption published in *Bangor Daily News*, 3 September 1945: "Souvenirs of the far north were brought back from Hebron, Labrador, by S/Sgt. Alfred H. Shapiro, Cpl. Elwood H. Belsheim and Cpl. Joseph W. Barber, AACS radio operators who just returned from almost a year in isolation. Dressed in Eskimo parkas and a sealskin jacket, they are examining some of the articles they bought from the Eskimos." (Collection of Elwood Belsheim)

---

[12] This chapter is based on conversations, emails and letters with/from Elwood "Woody" Belsheim, February 2009–June 2012.

[13] Letter from British Mission Board of the Moravian Church to Rev. F.W. Peacock, dated September 11, 1945. Obtained from Prof. Hans J. Rollmann. Our best guess as to who the author of the letter is would be P. E. Birtill, the joint secretary.

[14] Hannie Hettasch Fitzgerald clarifies that it was the church bells that were rung, not the school bells.

CHAPTER 6

The Search for Renatus and Harriot

WOODY AND THE OTHER TWO RADIO OPERATORS were interviewed for an article published in a U.S. military newspaper soon after they returned to Dow Army Airfield near Bangor, Maine. They had stopped at Goose Bay on their way back to Maine and watched a movie, but it hadn't made an impression as they couldn't remember the name of it. Woody was credited with gaining "fluent command of the Labrador Eskimo dialect," as well as being the crew's barber. The article mentioned that the men brought home souvenirs, including an Eskimo parka, miniature kayak and comiak [sic], sealskin jackets and handbags, and ivory and whalebone carvings." ([Bangor Daily News?] 1945).

Woody had entered the service on November 12, 1942, rising from a private to a sergeant. He was discharged at Fort MacArthur in San Pedro, California on February 13, 1946. When he returned to the States, he found that the girls seemed so phony with their red lips and made-up faces. But he got used to it. He went to work the very next day and writes that "my life since then has been as normal as most. The war was rarely discussed. We just enjoyed life, and one-by-one, we married and raised our families." (Belsheim 2010).

Fig. 48 Three weathermen upon returning to the USA.
S/Sgt. Alfred H. Shapiro, Cpl. Elwood H. Belsheim and Cpl. Joseph W. Barber.
(Collection of Elwood Belsheim, 1945)

Woody was 87 years old when we began talking about Hebron. He wanted to know what had happened to Harriot, and after hearing his stories, so did I. Looking at the kayak Renatus had made, only increased my desire to trace its origins. Sixty years was a long time, and it seemed almost a fool's errand to try, but every door I knocked on during the search opened.

The only thing I had to go on were the 1945 census records, available online. Woody had found those records, but nothing more. According to the census, Renatus and Loida had had four children. Paulina was already married and living with her husband, but Harriot, 18, Josef Richard, 13, Hulda, 10, Sabina, 4, were still at home. Josef Kefas Andreas, Harriot's 6-month-old son, who had been adopted by Renatus and Loida, was also living with them (Newfoundland Department of Public Health and Welfare, 1937).

I tried to find the Tuglavina family by researching more recent census records at Library and Archives Canada in Ottawa, but Newfoundland and Labrador had confederated with Canada in 1949, and Canadian law doesn't allow disclosure of personal information from censuses taken after 1921, so nothing was available. The Archives had interesting material on Hebron and Siegfried Hettasch, much of it about the relocation of Hebron Inuit to Nain and Makkovik in 1958–1959, but there was no clue as to how to find Renatus' family.

W. A. B. (Alec) Douglas, the military historian who helped discover the unmanned German weather station in Martin Bay, Labrador, was volunteering at the Canadian War Museum when I visited. Our conversation about the American presence in Hebron was news to him. There was no information regarding the weather station or G.I.'s in Hebron in their collections. Historians and archaeologists I had spoken to recognized that there had been some sort of buildings in Hebron, and they suggested they were military in origin, but didn't know what or whose it was.

Finally, a librarian at Library and Archives Canada suggested that Hans J. Rollmann, a Professor of Religious Studies at Memorial University of Newfoundland, might be able to help. So, I sent Prof. Rollmann an email asking whether he knew where I might find the Moravian Church records for Hebron. He replied the same day saying he had them in his office.

In short order, I was on my way to St. John's, Newfoundland, to search the Moravian church books and Periodical Accounts for news of Renatus and Harriot. All I found was tragedy.

An Untimely Death

Once World War II had ended, prospectors and geologists were commissioned by the Department of Natural Resources to survey the coast of Labrador for mineral deposits.

Fig. 49 Ramah, Labrador.
(Photo: Rozanne Enerson Junker, 2011)

Renatus, an experienced navigator, expert boatman, and English speaker, because of the time he had spent working for the British survey crew, was asked to pilot one of the boats north to Ramah in July 1946. He knew the area well as it was close to where Loida, his wife, had been born. There, they ran into pack ice, dangerous ice that isn't attached to land but floats along the coast in great masses, which interrupted their trip.

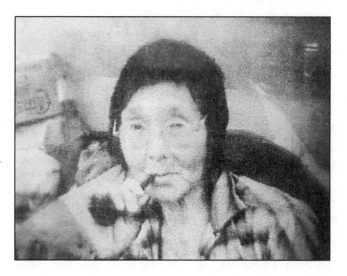

Fig. 50 Loida Semigak Tuglavina Henoche.
(Published with the permission of Stonia Nochasak)

After some weeks, Renatus was brought home severely ill with double pneumonia. Siegfried Hettasch wrote in the Periodical Accounts for 1945 that, "Not long after his arrival here, Renatus was called Home, passing away in an unconscious state. Renatus has been a noted person here at Hebron, having been a Church elder for a number of years, and despite his many mistakes and failings he was quite a good leader to his people, and a man with whom one was able to talk reason. We are all sorry to lose him." (Hettasch 1947: 42).

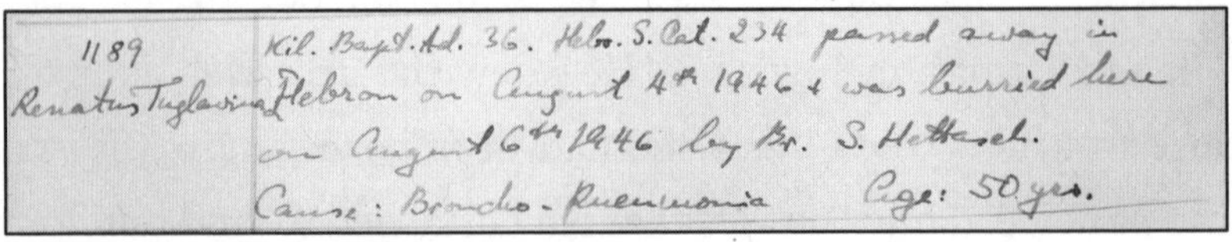
1189 Kil. Bapt. Ad. 36. Hebr. S. Cat. 234 passed away in
Renatus Tuglavina Hebron on August 4th 1946 & was buried here
on August 6th 1946 by Br. S. Hettasch.
Cause: Broncho-Pneumonia Age: 50 yrs.

Fig. 51 Death record of Renatus Tuglavina.
Hebron Church Book. (Microfilm 592 CNSA)

Renatus Tuglavina died on August 4, 1946, less than a year after Woody left Hebron. He was buried in a church service led by Siegfried Hettasch, two days later. He was 50 years old (Hebron CNSA: 1189). Loida was now alone with five children at home—Harriot (18), Josef (13), Sabina (4), Hulda (10) and Harriot's son, Josef (6 months).

The records provided a brief outline of Harriot's life, but they added little in the way of understanding her as a person. It was Woody's comment of Harriot being such a wonderful person that stayed with me. According to mission records, at the age of 21, she and her older sister Paulina (now widowed) were confirmed in the Moravian Church on Palm Sunday, March 30, 1947. (Hebron CNSA: Confirmation Record #740). Harriot's second child, Lena Louisa Elsie Dina Tuglavina, was born seven months later, on October 30, 1947.

Traditionally, Inuit girls were wed when they reached puberty. While the Moravians were able to establish a minimum marriage age, they were unsuccessful in stopping young people from doing what came naturally. Children were considered a blessing in Inuit families, especially because of the high infant mortality rate. The idea of an illegitimate child, or an unwanted child, did not exist. Families had a long-held system that determined which of the child's maternal relatives would be given the opportunity to adopt. In this case, the child's maternal grandmother had the first right. Thus, Loida and Renatus adopted Harriot's first child, Josef. Johannes and Sabina Tuglavina baptized Lena after adoption on November 9, 1947 (Hebron CNSA: #1199). Sabina was Loida's sister and Harriot's aunt. (Ben-Dor 1966: 67–68).

Harriot married Martin Semigak in a public service conducted by F. C. Paul Grubb on April 7, 1948, six months after Lena was born. The records identify Harriot as a spinster and Martin, a bachelor. Both were 21 years old. William Onalik and Jerry Nochasak were witnesses (Hebron CNSA: 392).

Harriot and Martin had two children. Dina Harriot Maggie Paulina Elizabeth was born at Iterungnek, their winter camp, on the fjord just north of Hebron, on December 15, 1950, and was baptized by F. C. Paul Grubb at a special service on January 28, 1951 (Hebron CNSA: 1249). Two years later, Harriot died during the birth of their second child, Jonas Gustave Thomas Semigak, also at Iterungnek, March 12, 1953. She was not yet 27 years old. She was taken back to Hebron and buried on March 19, in a service also conducted by F. C. Paul Grubb (Hebron CNSA: 889).

Four months later, on July 15, 1953, baby Jonas died in Saglek Bay of whooping cough, a bacterial infection, and enteritis, an inflammation of the small intestine caused by eating food or drinking liquids contaminated with bacteria or viruses. Wilson Semigak buried Jonas the same day. The missionaries, who diagnosed his conditions after the fact, recorded the event (Hebron CNSA: 1279).

Woody hadn't expected to find Renatus alive, but there was some thought that Harriot, being five years younger than him, might be. When learning she had died at such a young age, in childbirth, he simply said, "Then her children will never know what a kind person she was." (Belsheim 2011). So, the search for Harriot shifted to a search for her remaining children, a search complicated by the fact that there had been a total, some argue forced, relocation of Hebron Inuit in 1959.

Relocation Trauma

Relocation was a perfect storm. All the non-Inuit interests in Hebron—the governmental, religious and medical powers that be—agreed that closing Hebron, and moving the Inuit south, would be the best for all concerned. In early 1959, Walter Rockwood of the Division of Northern Labrador Affairs, which had replaced the Northern Labrador Trading Organization in 1951; Dr. W. A. Paddon from the International Grenfell Association, which provided medical treatment in Labrador; F. W. Peacock, Superintendent of the Moravian mission in Labrador; and missionary F. C. Paul Grubb agreed that it was impossible to maintain their presence in Hebron. They argued that financial, medical and economic conditions made their continued presence untenable (Grubb ca. 1957, MHA; Paddon ca. 1957, MHA; Peacock ca. 1957, MHA).

Paddon was adamant that Hebron was "unfit for human habitation. Existence pauperizing the people of Hebron, wasting money and resources." (Paddon ca. 1957, MHA). Grubb was more circumspect, writing that "this [is a] complicated matter. As general [Hebron] economy as good as any on Coast. But from health stand point and fuel [Hebron] is in very poor condition. But whole Northern Coast is very bad shape in regards to earning possibilities. These are reasons in very small nut shell." (Grubb ca. 1957, MHA).

Peacock cited lack of wood for fuel, Hebron's poor health (infant mortality rate "appallingly high" and tuberculosis also higher than other places on the coast), and the cost-saving nature of the measure. "If Hebron were closed the folk could be spread out among other villages to their own advantage to further education, to improve health and create better social conditions, it would be wise to close Hebron. Furthermore, to close Hebron would be to save man-power and money. The people of Hebron can never hope to make a decent living in their present community." (Peacock ca. 1957, MHA).

According to Carol Brice-Bennett, the rationale to relocate the Inuit south was made on six faulty assumptions, that: (1) houses, schools, and medical care were more important than the ability to make a living; (2) Inuit are all the same; (3) Inuit would be welcome and would integrate easily into new locations; (4) employment would be created; (5) there would be enough fish, seal, and food for all; and (6) the ecology of the new places would not be harmed (Brice-Bennett 1994b: 104–105).

They also failed to take into account that the area around Hebron had supported Inuit for hundreds of years.

The last Inuit boats left Hebron the weekend of October 8 and 9, 1959. As has been widely documented, relocation was disastrous for these Northern Inuit, with families and communities torn apart by prejudice, demoralization, hunger, dislocation, poverty and rootlessness that exist to this day. The Southern Inuit discriminated against the Hebron relocatees as they were darker and spoke a different language. Moreover, the Northerners no longer had hunting or sealing grounds to call their own, multiple families were crowded together in cobbled shacks, and even the food was not what they were used to.

Fig. 52 Residents leaving Hebron, 1959.
(Collection of the Hettasch Family, Labrador Institute, Happy-Valley Goose Bay)

As Ken Jararuse wrote in *Them Days*, "We thought we were being sent to better and happier places, but all we got was everything empty. We were hungry for country food: char, seals, birds which we never lacked while living at home in Hebron. This was the first time I had seen tears falling off my father's face. I was afraid of the light-coloured children who called us names and beat us up too many times. Life became hard for younger Inuit that tend to retaliate to situations that were forced upon them. Many turned to alcoholism and became suicidal. The police had their field day earning promotions and raises. There was murder, rapes and thievery by some who would not have done the same if not for the forced relocation. Once we moved we all received a criminal record." (Jararuse 2000: 61–65).

Years later Helge Ingstad who, along with his wife, the archaeologist Anne Stine Ingstad, discovered the Viking settlement L'Anse aux Meadows in Newfoundland noticed the difference: "The most interesting group were the Hebron Eskimoes, who had been moved south a short time ago when the mission in their area was closed down. There seemed to be a primitive forcefulness about these people, which was lacking in the others. They now live in small houses specially built for them, standing in a drab, city-like row; here young and old were ambling about seemingly without much purpose. These people do not freeze, they are not hungry, but it seems as if the joy of living has been extinguished in them. I talked with one of the older Eskimoes, and his eyes shone when time after time he reverted to his country away up north, with its endless coast and the splendid seal-hunting. They had accepted their destiny, as Eskimoes are wont to do, but their longing for their homeland will not soon be eradicated." (Ingstad 1969: 118).

Gary Baikie,[15] Superintendent at the Torngat Mountains National Park, summed up the tragedy this way, "Children of northern Inuit do not share their parents' memories of a better life, although many seem to have inherited the despair of dislocation." (Baikie in Evans 1999: 50).

The Search for Harriot's Family

I didn't have a lot of hope that I would be able to locate Harriot's children. Labrador was completely unknown territory for me and, with relocation, people moved from Hebron to Makkovik to Nain and who knew where else. Also, there were many who had the same name. I had found five or six Josef Tuglavina's in my church book search. At Prof. Rollmann's suggestion, I began to look for Harriot's children on Facebook as it seemed to be actively populated by Inuit young people. There I came across the poet Philip Igloliorte, the son of Dina Semigak whom I thought might be Harriot's daughter. When I connected with Philip, he said he had been placed in foster homes as a child, so he didn't know much about his birth family, but he put me in touch with his sister, Hulda Semigak, who lived in Happy Valley-Goose Bay, Labrador.

Hulda and I had exchanged numerous emails about the Tuglavina family when one day she wrote that it "hit her like a ton of bricks" when she realized that the Josef Kefas Andreas

Tuglavina I was looking for was the man she knew as Joe K. A., a name he used to differentiate himself from the many other Josef Tuglavina's in Labrador. Hulda said Joe K. A. had passed, but his wife, Ernestina, was still living in Nain. She wasn't sure about his sister Lena (Semigak H. 2010).

Fig. 53 Lena, her son Johannes and Emelia Townley.
(Collection of Henoche Townley)

While visiting Hulda in Happy Valley-Goose Bay, I also explored the archives of *Them Days*, an organization dedicated to collecting, protecting and promoting the stories of Labrador. I thought they might have a record of the existence of the secret American weather station in Hebron, but they didn't. I happened to mention to Aimee Chaulk, *Them Days* editor, that I had found Carol Brice-Bennett's work on Hebron and Hopedale extremely valuable, but that I had no idea how to get in touch with her. Aimee said "Oh! Carol, she lives right up the street!" (Chaulk 2011).

Fig. 54 Joe K. A. Tuglavina.
(Collection of Carol Brice-Bennett)

So, I called Carol that afternoon, and she was kind enough to rearrange her schedule so that we could have supper together. Seven hours later I had an enormous wealth of information to guide me in my search for Harriot's family. Carol had files of all of Harriot's four children. She shared photos she had taken of Joe K. A. Tuglavina and his cousin Elias "Jerry" Tuglavina. She also had the records of Renatus and Loida Tuglavina's births. The first thing Carol said to me when I told her what I was looking for was "What took you so long to find me?" (Brice-Bennett 2011).

Carol's research showed that Harriot's third child, Dina, died in Saglek Bay on May 22, 1955, two years after her mother and little baby brother, Jonas. Wilson Semigak buried her there the same day. Dina was only four years old, one of 15 Inuit who fell victim to the measles epidemic that year (Hebron CNSA: 1324).

At some point, perhaps after Renatus' death, Joe K. A. had gone to live with Johannes and Sabina Tuglavina, who had previously adopted his younger sister, Lena. The couple, who would have been in their early sixties at the time, never formally adopted him, nor were they the ones who baptized him, which troubled Joe K. A. greatly (Ben-Dor 1966: 135–137). Lena and Joe K. A. moved to Okak Bay and were then relocated to Makkovik with their foster parents.

When Lena was 21 years old, she married Timothy Townley. She died in Nain at the age of 35, on November 14, 1982, of severe trauma to the brain. The photo of her that I found in Nain is of a beautiful young woman, like her mother. Carol had not known Lena, but she had met Joe K. A. when she lived in Nain and had interviewed him for her work on relocation.

Carol also shared with me a photo of Elias "Jerry" Tuglavina, who was the son of Harriot's cousin, Hulda Tuglavina, and

Hank Bradley, the cook in Woody's unit. This was a surprise to Woody as he had been told that Hulda and her baby had both died in childbirth. A week before Woody passed away, he wrote me a letter to say that this Jerry must be someone else. And yet when I had spoken to Jerry a few months earlier in Nain, he told me his father was Hank Bradley and his mom, Hulda Tuglavina.

In Carol's interviews, Joe K. A. credits marrying his first cousin, Ernestina Loida Kristiana Basa Jararuse, the daughter of Harriot's sister Paulina, with saving his life. Like so many of his generation, torn from their homes and all they knew, relocation had been disastrous. Carol quotes Joe K. A. as saying: "We didn't know that place. We didn't know Makkovik. For me at least I got used to it, but I didn't want to live there. It's not my kind of place ... I didn't like *Kablunangajuks* (white settlers); I'm not used to them. I only talk Inuktitut. That's why I didn't want to live in Makkovik." (Brice-Bennett 1994a: 113, 153). Ernestina, who was born in Hebron February 16, 1952, was the sixth of Paulina's thirteen children. Ernestina was seven and Joe K. A. was a young teenager when they were relocated, Ernestina from Hebron and Joe K. A. from Okak.

Even though I had learned from Carol that all of Harriot's children had died, I still had my ticket to Nain (population 1400) so I thought I would try to find Ernestina, Renatus' niece. The flight was so cold that I kept my gloves and hat on the entire time. There was three feet of snow on the ground when I arrived at the Atsanik Lodge and it was well below zero and windy. Sharp nails were sticking up out of my windowsill. I didn't know why and I didn't think to ask.

I had earlier put announcements on the Inuit radio station, 99.9 FM, run by the OkâlaKatiget Society, requesting Ernestina to call me collect, but I hadn't heard anything from her. I didn't know whether she was still alive and, if so, where she was living. So, I talked with the desk clerk to see whether she had any idea how I might find her.

"Shouldn't be a problem," the clerk answered, "her daughter, Paula, works here in the morning."

Paula wasn't sure what to make of me the next day, but she agreed to tell her mom I was here.

A day later, I went to the OkâlaKatiget Society to search their archives and to meet their executive director, Sarah Leo. OkâlaKatiget is Inuktitut for *people who talk or communicate with each other*. The Society provides a regional, native communication service for those on the North Coast and the Lake Melville area of Labrador, and works to preserve and promote the language and culture of the Inuit within Nunatsiavut. I thought perhaps they could help me find other relatives of Renatus. I had the good fortune of telling the story of the kayak and my search for Renatus Tuglavina's family on the afternoon radio show hosted by Gordon Obed, Sr.

The next day, Tom Artiss, then a sociology graduate student at the University of Cambridge working on a treatise of Inuit music, took me by snowmobile to Ernestina's house where Paula made us tea. Ernestina and I talked like old friends, the wool blankets hung over the doors and wood stove kept us warm. We both cried when I showed her Carol Brice-Bennett's photo of Joe K. A. that I had downloaded on my laptop computer. She looked at the pictures of Woody and Harriot, but she was too young to remember either. I asked Ernestina if she knew who Joe K. A.'s father was but she shrugged her shoulders, which I interpreted to mean she didn't know or she didn't want to say.

Fig. 55 Ernestina Jararuse Tuglavina.
Singing *Aullagelaummiagame*, a song written for her by Joe K. A.
(Photo: Rozanne Enerson Junker, 2011)

Ernestina and Joe K. A. had had seven children, six of whom were still alive. Paula, their youngest, was living at home. Joe K. A. had died in 1996, at the age of 51, of cancer abetted by alcoholism. When Ernestina came by the hotel the next day, she told me about her parents, her father's death from drowning, her time in mission school with Kate Hettasch as her teacher, and about how much she still missed her husband. She sang the love song, *Aullagelaummigame*, that Joe K. A. had written for her when he was in jail in St. John's.

Tom Artiss had collected a number of Joe K. A.'s recordings as part of his graduate work. Joe K. A. played the mouth harmonica, guitar and accordion. One of his songs, *Rosiakkulak*, was included on the now out-of-print album *Under the Labrador Sky*. Ernestina also played guitar and sang. I suggested that musical talent must run in the family as her grandfather, Renatus, had bought a mouth organ in Killinek on his way back from delivering the mail in 1927.

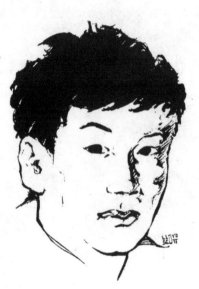

"Summer Day's"

The spring is ENDing again,
AND summer day,s will come again,
And the day,s be warm again.

The Summer day,s will be warm,
And the fall day,s be cold again,
I will be holding to my arm,
When It's get very cold again.

The rain will make the water
So well have Lot of blue Berrie's
The flower Like the water
So thus the nice real Red Berrie's

Summer day,s is coming again
And the rain will droping again
And summer day,s be warm again

by
Song Poem Author
Joe K. A. Tuglavina

Fig. 56 Joe K. A.'s song poem.
drawing of Joe K. A. by Lloyd Scott. Outdoorsman Magazine, 1968.

Just recently, a librarian at Memorial University found a line drawing of Joe K. A.'s face along with a "song poem" that he had written and published in the magazine *Outdoorsman* in 1968 (Outdoorsman. 1968: 31). At the time, Joe K. A. was taking pottery classes in Corner Brook, Newfoundland. The song poem was titled *Summer Day's*.

It was a surprise to learn that Harriot's younger sister, Hulda, was still living in Nain. The next day, Christine Baikie was kind enough to take me to visit her and her husband, Sem Kajuaksiak.

Fig. 57 Hulda Tuglavina Kajuatsiak.
(Photo: Rozanne Enerson Junker, 2010)

In her late seventies, Christine was still driving her own snowmobile. She translated Sem's Inuktitut into English for me. Sem, as it turned out, had been fishing with Woody and Renatus and smiled when he remembered being one of the three or four local Inuit on the trip from Hebron down to Nain with Renatus in the spring of 1945. Their son, David Renatus or Renie, who was ill at the time, was living with them.

Fig. 58 Sem Kajuatsiak.
(Photo: Rozanne Enerson Junker, 2010)

I also ran into Jerry Tuglavina, whom I had first met in Hebron in 2008 when he had the unimaginable job of trying to restore, or at least make an effort to stop, the disintegration of, the Moravian mission buildings. I had no inkling then that Woody had known both his parents. Jerry (Jeremias Elias Andreas) was born on December 8, 1945, two months after his father had been sent back to the U.S. with Woody. His mother had told him his father's name, but Woody had not shared that information with me. Jerry would have liked to have known his dad, and wondered whether he had any sisters or brothers, aunts or uncles.

After Nain, I flew to Hopedale as I had found out that Harriot's youngest sister, Sabina, was living there. I checked into the Amaguk Inn in Hopedale for three nights. While having breakfast the next morning, I learned that the Inn's cook, Irene, was from Hebron. It turned out that her parents were John and Eugenia Piercy, who had run the Labrador government store during the time Woody was there. I showed her the photograph that Woody had taken of her parents as a young couple, and later sent her a copy.

David Igloliorte, the heritage interpreter of the Hopedale Moravian Mission Complex, took me to meet Harriot's youngest sister, Sabina Rhoda Tuglavina Winters, a tiny woman with a green thumb. Woody had remembered Sabina as a beautiful four-year-old. Sabina was surprised and delighted to see the photos of herself as a young girl in Hebron that I had found during my searching.

The next day around 10:30 a.m. Gustav Semigak knocked on the door of my room. His wife, Lena, worked in the Inn's restaurant and she had told him I was looking for the family of Renatus Tuglavina. Gus had been one of Joe K. A.'s closest friends. He spoke of the difficulty of relocation, of living in a tiny room with many adults, of tears in his father's eyes, of seeing things a child should not have seen. He told me that he and Joe K. A. had spent time in jails together: "St. John's, Corner Brook. We hated white people and they hated us and we all did a lot of fighting, but we got blamed." (Semigak G. 2011).

Fig. 59 Sabina and her husband Henry Winters.
(Photo: Rozanne Enerson Junker, 2010)

Fig. 60 Gustav Semigak.
(Photo: Rozanne Enerson Junker, 2010)

Unlike Joe K. A., Gus had survived. He and his wife raised five children. He was a carpenter and fisherman, and was now training as an interpreter. As he walked me through the back pages of Brice-Bennett's book *Reconciling with Memories* (Brice-Bennett 1994b), Gus pointed to William Onalik's name and said "That's Joe K. A.'s father." (Semigak G. 2011). The same man who had been a witness at Harriot and Martin's wedding.

I hadn't told him I was looking.

---

[15] Baikie was also former director of the Torngâsok Cultural Centre in Nain and past secretary-treasurer of the Labrador Inuit Association.

CHAPTER 7

End of the Journey

RESEARCHING THE SEALSKIN KAYAK had taken me on an amazing journey I could never have imagined. It had provided a glimpse into a tiny slice of life—a year when a young American G.I. dropped into the life of Renatus Tuglavina and his family. And Renatus' family dropped into his, creating a year of experiences and adventures that he had held on to for 65 years.

I returned to Hebron aboard the *Clipper Adventurer* in 2011, this time with the knowledge of the American weather station and Renatus' family. I explored the remains of the sod houses, hollow overgrown indentations in the land, wondering which one belonged to the Tuglavina family. Woody would have known.

Of the American weather station, the most poignant reminder was a large metal eye threaded into a rock through which the cables had been strung to keep the buildings from blowing away. The four structures were long gone, salvaged, no doubt. But the metal eye remained firmly embedded.

Fig. 61 Standing at the weather station's location, Hebron.
(Photo: Rozanne Enerson Junker, 2011)

Fig. 62 Rusted out barrels from weather station, Hebron.
(Photo: Rozanne Enerson Junker, 2011)

Fig. 63 Cables used to keep the buildings from blowing away.
(Photo: Rozanne Enerson Junker, 2011)

Fig. 64 Weather station's old cook stove, Hebron.
(Photo: Rozanne Enerson Junker, 2011)

Fig. 65 Only rust remains, Hebron.
(Photo: Rozanne Enerson Junker, 2011)

When I began this search, the secret weather station in Hebron was but a distant memory of a few living American servicemen like Woody and a few Inuit, such as Sem Kajuatsiak, who had called Hebron home at the time. *Highways in the Sky: the Story of the AACS* didn't mention it. Neither did the American Legion's Fort Pepperrell Post #9 include it in their historical review of United States Military in Newfoundland and Labrador, 1941-1988 (United States Military in Newfoundland and Labrador 1988, TDA). A 1973 fire in the National Personnel Records Center in the U.S. Government Archives housed in St. Louis, Missouri, destroyed 16–18 million World War II files. Historians and archaeologists working in Hebron had identified the remains of the station, but they didn't know what the "Eurocanadian or other non-indigenous building foundations" (Thomson 1991: 15) represented.

Renatus Tuglavina had left a legacy, well beyond the sealskin kayak model. Moravian missionaries, Hudson's Bay Company traders, a British Royal Navy Commander, a Scottish Admiral in the Royal Navy, two Royal Navy surveyors, a Newfoundland sealing captain and a young Royal Canadian Mounted Police officer had all recorded aspects of his life. Peter Evans suggests that the rebellion Renatus led against the HBC in Hebron was the impetus for the establishment of the Newfoundland Ranger Force, so as to better serve the rural northern communities. That may be so, but I would also argue that it was reinforced by Baker's memo to the Admiralty calling for an investigation.

Two photos exist, and possibly a third: Baker's pictures of Renatus building a snow house in 1934, and of him driving his komatik, and what I believe to be Renatus as a young boy in the photograph of Old Tuglavi's house in Killinek in Samuel King Hutton's *Among the Eskimos of Labrador*. When assembled, they provide a glimpse of a man who lived life large and was respected and admired by his peers—Inuit and non-Inuit alike. The last written item I found concerning Renatus was in the Hebron Moravian Mission ground rent receipt book. He had paid 10 cents for the ground rent of his igloo on April 28, 1945. (MG 17 D 2 LAC).

I was troubled by Renatus' death. I doubt his wife, Loida, received any compensation from the men who hired him. She was left with four children at home. However, she did remarry Dan Henoche, from Nain, after relocation from Hebron.

Harriot's death in childbirth was troubling, but easier to understand. Perhaps if she had been in Hebron she might have lived. It is impossible to know. Dina's and Jonas' deaths from measles and whooping cough as young children in the 1950s were, unfortunately, all too common. Lena's, at the age of 35, from head wounds, and Joe K. A.'s, at the age of 51, from cancer and alcoholism both reflected the trauma associated with relocation.

Woody died two months after I returned from meeting Harriot's sisters, Hulda and Sabina, one year to the day after he had given me the kayak. He went very quickly. I didn't have a chance to say goodbye or thank him for sharing his story with me. He was 89 years old. His questions had been answered, but I had so many more left to ask.

The poet Philip Igloliorte,[16] my first contact when I began this search, drowned a few years later in the Ottawa River. Sem Kajuatsiak and his son Renie have died, Renie of cancer. Harriot's sister, Hulda Kajuatsiak, had been moved from Nain to a care facility in Happy Valley-Goose Bay where she passed away in March 2016 at the age of 80. Sarah Leo left the Okâla-Katiget Society and, until 2016, served as President of Nunatsiavut (Our Beautiful Land), the homeland of Labrador Inuit. Joe K. A. and Ernestina Tuglavina's daughter Paula passed away in February 2017. Ernestina remarried. Sabina Rhoda (Tuglavina) and Henry Winters have also passed away.

Life carries on but stories are soon forgotten without a conscious effort to remember. Luckily, Renatus and Woody both have families to carry their stories forward. Renatus Tuglavina's family remains in Labrador while Woody

Belsheim's family is primarily in Nevada and California. There are grandchildren, great-grandchildren and great-great-grandchildren not to mention nieces and nephews with names like Tuglavina, Onalik, Lidd, Nochasak and Belsheim.

Fig. 66 Annie Lidd and her granddaughter.
Annie is the daughter of Renatus' son Josef. (Photo: Rozanne Enerson Junker, 2011)

Fig. 67 Gwendolyn Tuglavina and Elias "Jerry" Tuglavina.
Father and daugher. (Photo: Rozanne Enerson Junker, 2011)

Renatus and Woody's stories would have been lost if I had not followed a whim and stopped by to visit Ida and Woody Belsheim on my way up to Eugene, Oregon. Renatus' kayak had taken me across Canada and back many times, over 25 000 km, and introduced me to people whose history and life experiences were exceedingly different from my own, and yet I found we were united by a common humanity.

The last person I met as part of this story was Hans-Ludwig Blohm, a well-known Canadian photographer and recipient of the Order of Canada. As a young 16-year-old school boy, lived underground in a German bunker at the end of the War and, in addition to his homework, fed ammunition into anti-aircraft guns aiming to shoot down Ferry Command planes. "But there were just too many of them," Blohm said (Blohm 2014).

Renatus' Kayak: A Labrador Inuk, An American G.I. and a Secret WWII Weather Station was a story waiting to be told, and I happened to be in the right place at the right time. And listened. I can only hope that for the family of Renatus Tuglavina and the people of Labrador, it will be a reminder of the bravery, courage and ingenuity of their ancestors. And for Woody and his family, a memory of a man full of warmth, curiosity, a willingness to explore and a desire to serve.

I am grateful that he kept, and honoured, the sealskin kayak. It truly is a gift of rememberance.

Fig. 68 Rozanne Enerson Junker and Johannes Lampe.
Nunatsiavut President Lampe holds Renatus' model kayak.
(Photo: Dave Lough, 2014)

---

[16] In 2009, Philip Igloliorte published a book entitled *Captured Moments* (Baico Publishing).

Afterword

I first met Rozanne in Nain in the summer of 2011 when she dropped by my office to see if any archaeological records existed for a secret American weather station at Hebron in northern Labrador. Being the location of a historic Labrador Inuit winter settlement, the site of a Moravian mission station established in 1830, and having been occupied over millennia by nearly every known cultural group to have ever lived in Labrador, there are lots of archaeological records for Hebron ... but there was nothing about the secret weather station.

I wondered if she was confused about the now famous, but once secret, Nazi German weather station a couple of hundred kilometers further north. It turns out that she was not confused, and information provided by her uncle Woody a few months later helped confirm that the remains of four structures located a few hundred meters north of the Moravian mission complex at Hebron were indeed those of the American weather station. These had been documented by archaeologists in 1991, but until 2011, the nature of these structures was not understood.

That day, I learned a little about Rozanne's story – that she had come all the way to northern Labrador from California to meet members of the Tuglavina family. During the course of her stay in the community, and in the weeks after, I learned more about what brought her to Nain. As she puts it, she had been brought by a sealskin kayak model, handmade by Renatus Tuglavina in 1944. Over six decades old, it was a Labrador style, skin-on-frame kayak model.

Tom Artiss, the graduate student who gave Rozanne a ride on a snowmobile to a house in Nain to meet Renatus' granddaughter, aptly described this tale as something straight out of Hollywood. The shaman Tuglavina, who lived in Labrador in the 18th century, were he here with us now, might describe the story as a series of events intentionally shaped by Renatus who set them in motion with an object of power ... "a gift of remembrance."

Rozanne's uncle Woody, and Renatus' daughter Harriot made a connection that lasted a lifetime ... indeed more than a lifetime. Rozanne's serendipitous visit with her uncle Woody and aunt Ida, Woody's stories and his decision to give Rozanne the kayak that he had kept safe for all those years have linked lives across generations, across oceans and international borders, and over more than seven decades of time.

As an archaeologist, I am intrigued by the centrality of the kayak to the story. Archaeology is a practice obsessed with objects, to the point that it has been called "the Discipline of Things" (Olsen et al. 2012). This obsession has for many years been a source of embarrassment for practitioners, who have felt the need to downplay the focus on artifacts and to emphasize the fact that what we are really interested in is people.

For instance, in an obituary for the great Australian archaeologist Vere Gordon Childe, who had been director of the Institute for Archaeology in London, and who has been referred to as the "greatest prehistorian in Britain, and probably the world" (Trigger 1980:11), Robert Braidwood famously wrote that he "never forgot the Indian behind the artifact" (Braidwood 1958:734). Though Braidwood's language would be considered far from politically correct today, the idea he was expressing has dominated archaeology since at least the early 1950s.

Stephen Loring, a great American archaeologist who has spent his career working in Labrador wrote much more recently that we need to "... remember that we are talking about people even though we call them projectile points" (Loring 1992:511). Similar positions in recent decades have led to a tremendous shift in focus in the heritage world towards the *intangible* which, many felt, had long been ignored.

Braidwood, Loring, and the countless others who have echoed the same sentiments were of course correct in a sense—the discipline is all about people after all. But our things are, quite literally, part of us ... we cannot live without them. As Haraway put it, "we are cyborgs" (1991:292), and as Olsen et al. have stated "we have always been cyborgs" (Olsen et al. 2012:133). There is, therefore, something to be said for the tangible, something which cannot be ignored, and quite recently, a handful of archaeologists have begun to openly and unabashedly embrace their obsession with objects, and to encourage their colleagues to do so as well (Olsen et al. 2012).

Labrador Inuit have certainly attached great importance to the tangible. The recognition of Inuit rights over things like archaeological material and Inuit cultural material were critical issues throughout negotiations between Labrador Inuit and the federal and provincial governments in relation to land claims and self-governance that took place between the 1970s and the early 2000s. Today these rights are constitutionally protected and make up a significant portion of an entire chapter devoted to archaeology in the *Labrador Inuit Lands Claims Agreement* (being schedule to S.N.L. 2004 c.L3.1).

Rozanne writes of the enormous responsibility she felt with the kayak that Woody had given her in the back of her car. She refers to it as a cultural treasure that she will return to Labrador if at all possible. Speaking once more of serendipity, or of fate, Labrador Inuit have been working towards the construction of a cultural center in Nain for the past 40 years. It just so happens that the centre, now known as *Illusuak*, which means sod house, is expected to open in the fall of 2017, with permanent exhibits set to be unveiled in the fall of 2018. There will be a place for Renatus' kayak in this centre. It is indeed, as Rozanne wrote, a cultural treasure, and one that has exponentially increased in value as a result of the story she has documented here. Not in monetary value, but in terms of interpretive value, and more importantly in terms of human connections and relationships through time and space.

Renatus' Kayak is so special as we now know so much about its context, and because it is the original, the real thing. The kayak and these stories have brought people together after more than 65 years, and I think they will continue to do so. Whether this is the stuff of Hollywood, of magic, serendipity, or fate, it is a story Rozanne was chosen to tell.

Jamie Brake
Archaeologist, Nunatsiavut Government
September 2017
Nain, Labrador

Fig. 69 Cairn at St. John's Harbour, Saglek Fjord.
(Photo: Rozanne Enerson Junker, 2011)

Bibliography

Archival Sources

**CNSA – Centre for Newfoundland Studies Archives–
Memorial University, St. John's, NL**

Canadian Dominion Bureau of Statistics. 1949. Eleventh census
   of Newfoundland and Labrador, 1945 — Labrador District —
   Saglak Bay to Narpertokh Bay. Available on the Newfoundland Grand Banks Genealogy Site at:
   <http://ngb.chebucto.org/C1945/45-hebron-lab.shtml> [Ac-
   cessed April 24, 2017]

Microfilm 592 – Kirchen buch dermission der Evangelischen
   brüder zu Hebron, Okak. *B. Kinder esk. Eltern.* p. 107 Nfld.

Microfilm 591 – Kirchen buch der genuine Hoffenthal
   (Hopedale), Ramah, Zoar, Killinek. Nfld.

Newfoundland Department of Public Health and Welfare, 1937.
   Census of Newfoundland and Labrador, 1935, Vol. 1: population by districts and settlements. St. John's, NL. CNS
   Microfilm 580 or hardcopy. Also available on the Newfoundland Grand Banks Genealogy Site at:

< http://ngb.chebucto.org/C1935/35-hebron-lab.shtml> [Accessed May 27, 2017]

CWM – Canadian War Museum–George Metcalf Archival Collection, Ottawa, ON

Clarke, James Y. No date. WWII German Automatic Weather Station—Labrador Coast, 20060203-001, 58A1, 243.1.

Mercer, F. G., 1972. Labrador in Retrospect. *RCMP Newsletter*, October 1972, 3–5. 20060203-001,243.2.

Peacock, F. W., 1982. Letter to Dr. W. A. B. Douglas, April 7, 1982. 20060203-001, 243.3.

HBC – Archives of Manitoba–Hudson's Bay Company Archives, Winnipeg, MB

B.418/a/1–3 – Hebron Post Journals 1926–1942 (Reel 1MA29).

B.466/1/1–15 – Port Burwell Post Journal 1920–1939 (Reel 1MA55).

HFC – Hettasch Family Collections (Collection 249) – Archives and Special Collections – Queen Elizabeth II Library —Memorial University of Newfoundland — St. John's, NL

Glaser, Jan. 1945. Letter to Frieda and Siegfried Hettasch. August 7, 1945.

Hettasch, Siegfried. 1945. Letter to Rev. William Peacock. 23 Mar. 1945. Manuscript.

White, Linda, 2005. Hettasch Family Collection Historical Background.

LAC – Library and Archives Canada, Ottawa, ON

Peacock, F.W. 1944. *Letter to Richard White*, June 21, 1944. Richard White Fonds. R11967-3-3-E.

MG 17 D 2 – Receipt for Ground Rent (1945-1955).

MHA – Maritime History Archive —Memorial University of Newfoundland — St. John's, NL

Grubb, F. C. Paul. ca 1957. Forms Requesting Resettlement.

Paddon, W. A. ca. 1957. Forms Requesting Resettlement.

Peacock, F. W. ca. 1957. Forms Requesting Resettlement.

The above three documents are available at: <https://www.mun.ca/mha/resettlement/documents_full_vie w.php?img=023_circulars&galleryID=Doc1> [Accessed April 24, 2017]

TDA – Them Days Archive–Happy Valley-Goose Bay, NL

United States Military in Newfoundland and Labrador, 1988. *American Legion Ft. Pepperrell Post #9 Historical Review 1941-1988. Part 1.* St. John's, NL. PL 442

Air University (U.S.). 1943. *Living off the Arctic. Informational Bulletin.* Eglin Field, Florida: Arctic, Desert, and Tropic Information Center. July 1, 1943. A.6.

TRC – The Rooms Corporation of Newfoundland and Labrador–Provincial Archives Division, St. John's, NL

Anderson, D. Murray. 1935. Letter to J. B. Thomas, April 15, 1935. GN 2.5.645

Baker, E. H. B. 1934. Report [to the Admiralty] on the Journey to Hebron and the Investigation of the Trouble Among the Eskimos of that District, February 17, 1934. File 38, Box 224. GN13/1/B

Button, Maxwell. 1934. Letter to P. J. O'Neill, Esq. "Report on Condition of Esquimos in Labrador," 13/1/B, Box 453, #69.

Hopper, George D. 1943. "Memo to Wilfrid W. Woods," 19 June 1943, Public Utilities General, 1943-44, Box S5-1-2, File 4.

Parsons, Ralph, 1929. Memo to the Commissioner on Finance and the Colonial Secretary. December 2, 1929-June 25, 1929. GN 2.5.645.

Woods, Wilfrid W., 1943. Confidential Memorandum for the Commission of Government, 28 June 1943, Box S5-1-2, File 4, Public Utilities General, 1943–44.

USNA – US National Archives–Federal Register, Washington, D.C.

Roosevelt, Franklin Delano, 1942. *Executive Order No 9066.* February 21, 1942.

List of References

Amagoalik, John. 2001. "What is this Land?" in *Voice of the Natives: The Canadian North and Alaska.* Toronto: Penumbra Press.

Baker, E. H. B. 1934. *Private Diary, H.M.S. Challenger's Winter Survey Party (1933–1934).* Transcribed by Rozanne Enerson Junker. 2011. Unpublished.

[Bangor Daily News?]. 1945. "Three Arctic Veterans Now at Dow Field Draw First Pay in a Year" in *[Bangor Daily News?].* September 3.

Bassler, Gerhard. 2014. Vikings to U-Boats: The German Experience in Newfoundland and Labrador. Montréal: McGill-Queen's University Press.

Belsheim, Elwood "Woody". 2010. Conversations. (Personnal communication, May 3–5, 2010).

Belsheim, Elwood "Woody". 2011. Conversations. (Personnal communication, February 2011).

Ben-Dor, Shmuel. 1966. *Makkovik: Eskimos and Settlers in a Labrador Community; a Contrastive Study in Adaptation.* St. Johns: Institute of Social and Economic Research, Memorial University of Newfoundland. (Newfoundland Social and Economic Studies; 4)

Blohm, Hans-Ludwig. 2014. Conversation. (Personnal communication, January 23, 2014).

Braidwood, Robert John. 1958. "J. Vere Gordon Childe 1892–1957" in *American Anthropologist.* 60:733–736.

Brice-Bennett, Carol. 1994a. *Dispossessed: The Eviction of Inuit from Hebron, Labrador.* Happy Valley, NL: Labrador Institute of Northern Studies.

Brice-Bennett, Carol. 1994b. "The Redistribution of the Northern Labrador Inuit Population: A Strategy for Integration and Formula for Conflict" in *Zeitschrift fur Kanada-Studien.* [Augsburg, Germany]: Gesellschaft für Kanada-Studien [Association for Canadian Studies], 26.2:95–106

Brice-Bennett, Carol. 1996a. *Genealogy of Semigak.* "The Northlanders: A history of the population, socio-economic relations and cultural change of Inuit occupying the remote northern coast of Labrador." Unpublished paper.

Brice-Bennett, Carol. 1996b. *Genealogy of Tuglavina.* "The North-landers: A history of the population, socio-economic relations and cultural change of Inuit occupying the remote northern coast of Labrador." Unpublished paper.

Brice-Bennett, Carol. 2000. Reconciling with Memories: A Record of the Reunion at Hebron 40 Years after Relocation. Nain, NL: Labrador Inuit Association.

Brice-Bennett, Carol. 2003. *Hopedale: Three Ages of a Community in Northern Labrador.* St. John's, NL: Historic Sites Association of Newfoundland and Labrador.

Brice-Bennett, Carol. 2011. Conversation. (Personnal communication, February 19, 2011)

Brown, Stephen R. 2015. *White Eskimo: Knud Rasmussen's Fearless Journey into the Heart of the Arctic.* Madeira Park: Douglas and McIntyre.

Budgell, Leonard. 1990. "The Wonderful People of Hebron" in *Them Days.* Happy Valley-Goose Bay: *Them Days.* 15.2:54–63.

Budgell, Leonard, and Claudia Coutu Radmore. 2009. *Arctic Twilight: Leonard Budgell and Canada's Changing North.* Toronto: Blue Butterfly.

Butler, Kenneth C. 1963. *Igloo Killinek.* Toronto: Longman.

Canadian Dominion Bureau of Statistics. 1949. Eleventh census of Newfoundland and Labrador, 1945 — Labrador District — Saglak Bay to Narpertokh Bay. Available on the Newfoundland Grand Banks Genealogy Site at: <http://ngb.chebucto.org/C1945/45-hebron-lab.shtml> [Accessed April 24, 2017]

Cavalier Chronicle. 1940a. *Land is Purchased for Airplane Base in County*. January 5, 1940. Front page.

Cavalier Chronicle. 1940b. *Deliver Bombers to Canada at Border: Hauled Over Line At Pembina Port Monday*. January 19, 1940. Front page.

Chaulk, Aimee. 2011. Conversation. (Personnal communication, February 19, 2011).

Christie, Carl A. 1995. *Ocean Bridge: The History of RAF Ferry Command*. Toronto: University of Toronto Press.

Craven, Wesley Frank and James Lea Cate. 1955. *The Army Air Forces in World War II. Vol. VI: Men and Planes*. Chicago: University of Chicago Press.

Craven, Wesley Frank and James Lea Cate. 1958. *The Army Air Forces in World War II. Volume VII. Services Around the World*. [Chapters 11 and 12]. Chicago: University of Chicago Press. Available through the Ibiblio/HyperWar website. Accessed April 24, 2017. <https://www.ibiblio.org/hyperwar/AAF/VII/index.html>

Douglas, W. A. B. (Alec). 1982. "The Nazi Weather Station in Labrador." in *Canadian Geographic.* 101.6: 42–47.

Douglas, W. A. B. (Alec). 2011. Conversation. (Personnal communication, May 21, 2011).

Dzuiban, Stanley W. 1959. *U.S. Army in World War II.* Washington, D.C.: Office of the Chief of Military History.

Evans, Peter, ed. 1999. "How the North Was Lost: Hebron and Nutak Remembered." in *Kinatuinamut Ilingajuk.* Nain: Okâla-Katiget Society. 114.

Evans, Peter. 2011. Transformation of Indigenous Resistance and Identity in Northern Labrador. PhD diss. University of Cambridge.

Fitzhugh, Lynne D. 1999. The Labradorians: Voices from the Land of Cain. St. John's, NF: Breakwater.

Flanagan, Susan. 2016. "The Atlantic Charter." in Newfoundland Quarterly. 108(3):37–41.

Forbes, Alexander. 1932. "Surveying in Northern Labrador." in American Geographical Society. 22.1:30–60.

Grubb, F. M. 1943. "Hebron Annual Report, 1942." in Periodical Accounts of the Work of the Moravian Missions. Tytherton: Trust Society for the Furtherance of the Gospel. June 1943. 40–44.

Hampson, Thomas. 2005. "HMS Challenger's Wintering Party, 1933–1934: A Labrador Journal." in The Northern Mariner. Glover, William, ed. XV.1:27–74.

Haraway, Donna J. 1991. "A Cyborg Manifesto: Science, technology and socialist-feminism in the late twentieth century." in *Simians, Cyborgs and Women,* by Donna J. Haraway. Routledge, New York.

Harp, George. 1939. "Hebron Annual Report for 1938" in *Periodical Accounts of the Work of the Moravian Missions 120* (June 1939): 120–125.

Hettasch, Siegfried Paul. 1946. "Hebron Annual Report for 1945" in *Periodical Accounts of the Work of the Moravian Mission 154* (June 1946): 44–47.

Hettasch, Siegfried Paul. 1947. "Hebron Annual Report for 1946" in *Periodical Accounts of the Work of the Moravian Mission 155* (June 1947): 40–44.

Hettasch Fitzgerald, Johanna (Hannie). 2007. "Eulogy and Remembrance Tribute." *Moravian Church in Newfoundland and Labrador Blog.* December 15. Accessed April 24, 2017. <http://labradormoravian.blogspot.ca/2007/12/eulogy-and-remembrance-tribute.html >

Hettasch Fitzgerald, Johanna (Hannie). 2015. Conversation. (Personnal communication, November 15, 2015).

Higgins, Jenny. 2006. "Canadian Presence." *Newfoundland and Labrador Heritage* Web Site. Accessed April 24, 2017. <http://www.heritage.nf.ca/articles/politics/canadian-presence.php>

Horwood, Harold Andrew. 1986. *A History of the Newfoundland Ranger Force*. St. John's, Nfld.: Breakwater.

Hutton, Samuel King. 1912. *Among the Eskimos of Labrador*. Toronto: Musson Book Co.

Ingstad, Helge. 1969. *Westward to Vinland;* New York: St. Martin's.

Jararuse, Ken. 2000. "Hebron: My Childhood Days Remembered Very Briefly." in *Them Days* 25.2:60–64.

Jenkins, McKay. 2005. *Bloody Falls of the Coppermine*. New York: Random House.

Kaplan, Susan. 1980. "Neo-Eskimo Occupations of the Northern Labrador Coast." in *Arctic* 33.3:646–658.

Kean, Abram. 2000. *Old and Young Ahead;* St. John's, NL: Flanker Press Ltd.

Kennedy, John Charles. 1982. *Holding the Line: Ethnic Boundaries in a Northern Labrador Community*. St. John's, NL: Institute of Social and Economic Research, Memorial University of Newfoundland.

Kleivan, Helge. 1966. *The Eskimos of Northeast Labrador: A History of Eskimo-white Relations, 1771–1955.* Oslo: Norsk Polarinstitutt.

Loring, Stephen. 1992. *Prince and Princesses of Ragged Fame: Innu Archaeology and Ethnohistory in Labrador.* Unpublished PhD Dissertation, Department of Anthropology, University of Massachusetts, Amherst.

Loring, Stephen and Beatrix Arendt. 2009. "... they Gave Hebron, the City of Refuge ... (Joshua 21:13): An Archaeological Reconnaissance at Hebron, Labrador." in *Journal of the North Atlantic* 1:33–56.

Ludecke, Cornelia. 2005. "East Meets West: Meteorological Observations of the Moravians in Greenland and Labrador since the 18th Century." in *History of Meteorology* 2: 123-32.

Madsen, Gill R. 1946. *Historical Record for Month of December 1945.* [Unpublished report of an American serviceman in the 3rd rotation in Hebron, 1945–1946.]

McGhee, Robert. 2005. *The Last Imaginary Place: A Human History of the Arctic World.* Oxford: Oxford University Press.

McGrath, Darrin et al. 2005. *The Newfoundland Rangers.* St. John's, NL: DRC Publishing.

Moravian Church in North America. 2017. *A Brief History of the Moravian Church.* Accessed April 24, 2017.
<http://www.moravian.org/the-moravian-church/history/>

Neely, Harold L. 1968. "The Saglek Story, Arctic Tragedy in 1942." *Daedalus Flyer*, March 1968, VIII (1). Accessed April 24, 2017. <http://www.b26.com/page/saglek_story_artic_tragedy_1942.htm>

Olsen, Bjørnar, Michael Shanks, Timothy Webmoor and Christopher Witmore. 2012. *Archaeology: The Discipline of Things*. University of California Press, Berkeley.

Outdoorsman. 1968. "Meet Joe." in *Outdoorsman. Toronto: Pen-Reid Publications*. July-August.

Parsons, John. 2003. Probably without Equal: Frank Mercer and the Newfoundland Rangers. Shearstown, N.L.: Grassey Pond Pub.

Periodical Accounts. 1871. "Retrospect of the History of the Mission of the Brethren's Church in Labrador for the Past Hundred Years (1771–1871)." in Periodical Accounts relating to Moravian Missions 28: 1-19, 53-72.

Periodical Accounts. 1904. "Labrador — Extracts from the Station Diaries, July 1st, 1903—July 1st 1904. Ramah." in Periodical Accounts relating to Moravian Missions 60: 608–624.

Periodical Accounts. 1928. "Labrador–Hopedale." in Periodical Accounts Relating to Moravian Missions 136:236–249.

Ritchie, George Stephen. 1958. Challenger; the Life of a Survey Ship. New York: Abelard-Schuman.

Ritchie, George Stephen. 2011. Conversations. (Personnal communication, April 29, 2011, and May 2, 2011).

Rollmann, Hans J. 2002. *Labrador through Moravian Eyes: 250 Years of Art, Photographs & Records*. St. John's, Nfld.: Special Celebrations of Newfoundland and Labrador, Dept. of Tourism, Culture and Recreation.

Rollmann, Hans J. 2009. *Moravian Beginnings in Labrador: Papers from a Symposium Held in Makkovik and Hopedale*. St. John's, NL: Faculty of Arts Publications, Memorial University of Newfoundland.

Rollmann, Hans J. 2017. Email. (Personnal communication, January 13, 2017).

Roosevelt, Franklin D. 1940. *The Great Arsenal of Democracy, Radio Address, December 29, 1940*. Accessed April 24, 2017. <http://www.americanrhetoric.com/speeches/fdrarsenalofdemocracy.html>

Schledermann, Peter. 1996. *Voices in Stone: A Personal Journey into the Arctic past*. Calgary: Arctic Institute of North America of the University of Calgary.

Semigak, Gustav. 2011. Conversation. (Personnal communication, February 26, 2011).

Semigak, Hulda. 2010. Email. (Personnal communication, September 18, 2010).

Semigak, Hulda. 2011. Conversations. (Personnal communication, February 18–19, 2011).

Shores, Louis. 1947. *Highways in the Sky: The Story of the AACS;* New York: Barnes and Noble.

Smith, Gordon W. 2009. "Weather Stations in the Canadian North and Sovereignty." in *Journal of Military and Strategic Studies* 11(3):1–63.

Tanner, Väinö. 1947. *Outlines of the Geography, Life & Customs of Newfoundland-Labrador (the Eastern Part of the Labrador Peninsula) Based upon Observations Made during the Finland-Labrador Expedition in 1939, and upon Information Available in the Literature and Cartography.* Cambridge [England]: Cambridge University Press.

The Daily News. 1934. "Trial of Esquimaux On Board S.S. 'Kyle'" in *The Daily News.* St. John's. August 17. Front page.

Thompson, A. G. N. 1945. "The Shipwreck of the Iris" in [Aurora Borealis Arctic Yearbook], *Polar Airway to the Old World.* Hyde Park, MA: Tribune Publications. 24. [distributed free to personnel in Air Transport Service. Part of Elwood Belsheim personal papers]

Thomson, Callum. 1991. *Report of a Preliminary Archaeological Review of 8 Proposed Tourist Facility Sites in Northern Labrador.* S.l.: S.n.

Time Magazine. 1940. "Great Britain: Shirts On." in *Time.* September 16.

Trigger, Bruce G. 1980. *Gordon Childe: Revolutions in Archaeology.* London: Thames & Hudson.

Uboat.net 2017. *U-867.* Accessed April 24, 2017. <http://uboat.net/boats/u867.htm>

Walters, Raymond. 1952. *Weather Training in the AAF 1937–1945.* S.l.: Air University. (U.S. Air Force Historical Study, 56). Declassified. IAW EO12958, 1.

Wikipedia. 2017a. *German Sumarine U-537.* Accessed April 24, 2017. <https://en.wikipedia.org/wiki/German_submarine_U-537>

Wikipedia. 2017b. *Davis–Monthan Air Force Base.* Accessed April 24, 2017. <https://en.wikipedia.org/wiki/Davis–Monthan_Air_Force_Base>

Wikipedia. 2017c. *Renatus.* Accessed April 24, 2017. <https://en.wikipedia.org/wiki/Renatus>

Wilderness.net. 2017. *Mount Evans.* Accessed April 24, 2017. <http://www.wilderness.net/NWPS/wildView?WID=373>

Wyatt, A. G. N., 1934. "Surveying Cruises of H.M.S. Challenger off the Coast of Labrador in 1932 and 1933." in *The Geographical Journal* 84.1:33–53.

Index of People and
Place Names

Unless otherwise noted, communities are located in Newfoundland and Labrador. Page numbers in italics refer to end of chapter notes. Pages numbers in bold refer to illustrations and their captions.

Printed by Imprimerie Gauvin
Gatineau, Québec